What People Are Saying about the Book

A wonderful weekly reader, offering us a chance to discover a deep personal sense of meaning that ultimately expresses itself in acts of purpose.

Victoria Maizes, MD
Andrew Weil Endowed Chair in Integrative Medicine
Executive Director, Andrew Weil Center for Integrative Medicine
Professor of Clinical Medicine, Family Medicine and Public Health, University of Arizona

This beautiful collection, carefully curated by a master teacher, belongs on our nightstands, in our backpacks, anywhere it can be readily available as healing balm for our wounded souls. Week by week, we are led along a path towards resilience, self-nurturing and grateful living.

Marilyn Schlitz, PhD
CEO/President Emeritus and Senior Fellow at the Institute of Noetic Sciences
Author, *Living Deeply: The Art and Science of Transformation in Everyday Life; Consciousness and Healing: Integral Approaches to Mind Body Medicine;* and *Death Makes Life Possible*

There is nothing usual or ordinary about Fred Craigie's rich, compelling invitation to explore who we are and what matters to us. It's insanely readable, this beautifully organized mashup of poetry, philosophy, psychology and spirituality.

Belleruth Naparstek, ACSW, BCD
Author of *Invisible Heroes: Survivors of Trauma and How They Heal*; and Publisher of the Health Journeys guided imagery & meditation audio collection

In this book, Fred Craigie has compiled a treasure trove of humane and timeless wisdom. Informational and inspirational, these meditations will assist you in living joyfully, meaningfully, and gracefully. Reading it was a true gift.

Robert Emmons, PhD
Professor of Psychology,
University of California, Davis.
Editor-in-Chief of *The Journal of Positive Psychology* and author of *Thanks! How Practicing Gratitude Can Make You Happier, Gratitude Works!* and *The Little Book of Gratitude.*

This book is truly a gift - a beautiful guide to infusing our daily lives with greater happiness, insight, and tranquility.

Lise Alschuler, ND, FABNO
Associate Director, Fellowship in Integrative Medicine
Professor of Clinical Medicine - College of Medicine, University of Arizona

Inspiration and spirituality come into our lives in many ways with Weekly Soul. *This treasure of a book will surely be dog-eared and treasured throughout the 52 weeks of the year.*

Sharon Salzberg
author of Lovingkindness and Real Change

Dr. Craigie brings us deeper into the mystery of living with reverence and awe- the key to becoming more fully alive.

Dr. Ann Marie Chiasson
Associate Professor of Clinical Medicine,
Andrew Weil Center for Integrative Medicine,
University of Arizona, Tucson, Arizona

Weekly Soul

Fifty-two Meditations
on
Meaningful, Joyful, and Peaceful Living

Frederic C. Craigie, Jr., Ph.D.

To
Eunice
in honor of your own
spirituality and the legacy
of your contributions
in Nursing, ministry
and
compassionate relationships

Blessings,
Fred

September 2021

For information, contact
MSI Press
1760-F Airline Highway, #203
Hollister, CA 95023

Cover art, *The Birds, the Plants, Chanted and Danced,*
© Caren Loebel-Fried

The author gratefully acknowledges these sources for permission to reprint the following;

Excerpt from "The Real Work," from *Standing by Words,* © Copyright 1983 by Wendell Berry, reprinted by permission of Counterpoint Press.

Excerpt from *Spirituality and Health Care: Reaching Toward a Holistic future* (© 2000, The Park Ridge Center for the Study of Health, Faith and Ethics) by Jack Shea, STD, reprinted by permission of the author.

Excerpt from *The Mindful Path to Self-Compassion* (© 2009, Guilford Press) by Christopher Germer, Ph.D., reprinted by permission of the author.

LCCN: 2020918223

ISBN: 978-1-950328-47-5

To Beth

The journey with you has been
such a blessing for all these years.

Frederic C. Craigie, Jr., Ph.D.

Contents

Frederic C. Craigie, Jr., Ph.D.

Acknowledgments

As I think about the evolution of this book, I smile in gratefulness for the contributions of so many people to the formation of these ideas and to my own spiritual journey.

Ed and Jan Berger are long-time friends, colleagues, and recipients of my weekly reflections. Ed suggested many years ago, "You should write a book based on those quotations." Thanks, Ed. Here it is.

My colleagues at the Andrew Weil Center for Integrative Medicine at the University of Arizona College of Medicine have been partners in rich dialogues about wellness and healing, and been a constant source of support and encouragement. Among the many people at the Weil Center who I have been blessed to know over the years, the colleagues with whom I have worked most closely in recent times have been Victoria Maizes, MD, Rocky Crocker, MD, Priscilla Abercrombie, RN, NP, PhD, Molly Burke, MFA, Devorah Coryell, Ann Marie Chiasson, MD, MPH, CCFP, Lise Alschuler, ND, Amy Williams, Morgan Gasho, Rosalyn dePalo, MPH, Kathryn Durban, and Karen Mihina. Thanks to Andrew Weil, MD, for his visionary leadership in the evolution of integrative, person-centered care. My friend Belleruth Naparstek, ACSW, BCD, is a fellow outlander, teaching from Ohio as I often do from Maine, and enlivens my own spirit with her practical wisdom and timely humor. The hundreds of students in the integrative medicine programs... physicians, nurse practitioners, nurses, acupuncturists, social workers, an occasional psychologist, and many others... have my respect for charting new directions in health care, and have very often been my teachers with their stories and experiences.

Thanks especially to Priscilla Abercrombie for her friendship and for the beautiful Foreword.

The particular story in the Civility chapter, generously shared by nurse practitioner Julie M Bosch, PhD, ARNP, Lt Col (retired) USAF, will inspire readers to honor the sacred commitments of their lives, even in the midst of grave personal affronts.

The presenters and participants at the Thomas Nevola, MD, Symposium on Spirituality and Health, the oldest nonsectarian symposium on spiritualty and health in the United States, have been a remarkable and engaging community. I am privileged to have had continuing relationships with a number of our principal presenters, among them, Christina Puchalski, MD, Patricia Mathes Cane, PhD, Lisa Miller, PhD, Robert Emmons, PhD, Sharon Salzberg, and Carolyn Lukensmeyer, PhD. Gratefulness especially for my close colleagues in planning these symposia in recent years; Beth Craigie, Susan Cross, RN, Lisa Hickey, LCSW, CCS, Barbara Moss, DO, MPH, Joy Anne Osterhout, MS, MCHES, RYT, and the indispensable, unbelievably organized, and ever-cheerful Ann Byron.

Two thousand people receive my weekly reflections, and I so much appreciate the kindness of many people each week to write short notes of response. I am indebted, I should also say, for the life experiences and wisdom of the fifty-two people quoted in this book, and for all of the authors and commentators whose ideas I have shared in these reflections since 2004.

The folks at MSI/San Juan have been delightful partners in publishing this book. Betty Lou Leaver, PhD, Carl Leaver and colleagues clearly take great pride in their work and in their professional and personally-engaged relationships with authors. Their organization is as much a community, as it is a business.

The gorgeous image that graces the cover of the book is a block print from Caren Ke´ala Loebel-Fried. Based in Hawaii, Caren is an artist and author who holds special passion for the celebration and conservation of the beauty in the natural world, and for Hawaiian cultural traditions. The print is The Birds, the Plants, Chanted and Danced. It is inspired by the Hawaiian creation story of Keaomelemele, embracing dance, chant and nature. To me, it represents community and joy. You can see more about Caren and her beautiful work at www.carenloebelfried.com.

Fred Frawley, distinguished Maine attorney and fellow Dartmouth graduate, helped me in thinking about intellectual property and permissions. Bill O'Hanlon, MS, years ago, helped in my transition from writing solid but sonorous journal articles to writing books that people might actually read. Douglas Harper has done incredible work with his online etymology dictionary, to which I often turn for a richer understanding of words, and has graciously given his permission to cite his material. Jeff Matranga, PhD and Jeri Wilson, E-RYT-500, have been friends, fellow professionals, and significant contributors to the landscape of health and wellness in Central Maine.

Our oldest friends as a couple, Charlie and Bob Jerard, remain close with us even across miles of separation. In seeing them, we are always uplifted and inspired as we share with one another the movement of Spirit in our lives.

Frederic C. Craigie, Jr., Ph.D.

My dear friend and colleague... and our adoptive sister... Persis Hope, FNP, teaches me about functional medicine, cooks some great whole-foods meals, shares in tracking the ups and downs of the Red Sox, and keeps me laughing.

I dedicated my 2010 book to our children, Heather, Matthew and Thomas Craigie, saying of them, "The spirit and commitments of your lives inspire me and make the world a better place." Ten years later, this is abundantly true. You are all engaged in work that has ripple effects on behalf of goodness, healing, justice, and sustainability in your communities and beyond, and the personal qualities that you show, day in and day out, remind us all about devotion, integrity, and love. The same is true for your remarkable partners, Matthew Burkhart, Alyssa Craigie, and Emily Craigie. And those six incredible grandchildren... Henry Burkhart, Lillian Craigie, Teo Burkhart, Olin Craigie, Romana Craigie, and Ari Craigie. You touch my heart, as you will touch the hearts of people whose lives join with yours in years to come. Not a day goes by that I don't think how incredibly blessed I am to have all of you in my life.

My wife, Beth, embodies the twelve qualities in this book as well as anyone I have ever met. I can't imagine a better life... richer and more joyful... than to be journeying along with her.

Foreword

Who would pass up an occasion to contemplate a more meaningful, joyful, and peaceful life?

Dr. Craigie offers us an opportunity to look within and explore critical questions such as, "Who am I?" "What is most important to me?" "What do I care utmost about?" "What brings meaning and joy to my life?"

As an integrative health coach, I ask each of my coaching partners these fundamental questions at the start of our work together. They center the encounter on what is important to the coaching partner so that as we work together we can align changes in health behaviors with the partner's core values.

Most people know what they need to do to be healthier, but they need to connect this to why they want to be healthier in order to make successful changes. Some people have not spent much time contemplating the why.

I cared for women as a nurse practitioner for over 30 years. Too often, I saw little change in health behaviors, some of which were extremely destructive because our health care system does not adequately center on each unique individual and on what is important to them. It was not until I became an integrative health coach that I began

Frederic C. Craigie, Jr., Ph.D.

to witness people making the transformative life changes needed to live a more healthful and meaningful life.

It is no wonder that I am drawn to the work of Dr. Craigie, a man who is a nationally recognized expert in spirituality in health care, and a dogged proponent of the exploration of the spirit in patient encounters and in health care institutions. His 2010 book, Positive Spirituality in Health Care, has been an essential body of knowledge for those who want a sensible approach to incorporating spirituality and personal values into health care. One can pick up the book and be guided through well-researched practical steps for exploring spirituality. It is just what those of us in health care need as the importance of spirituality is often not appreciated.

This book, Weekly Soul, is the logical next step for those who want to examine their own spirituality. To pick up this book is to undertake a personal journey. It is a chance to savor for a week an inspirational quote, read Fred's reflections on that quote, and to ponder a few stimulating questions that help you reflect on how the quote may be significant for you.

Mahatma Gandhi said, "If we could change ourselves, the tendencies in the world would also change. As a man changes his own nature, so does the attitude of the world change towards him." It is personal transformation that leads to societal change. That's why taking the time to digest the contents of this book and explore the questions it poses is so essential. For instance, the book raises questions such as, "How can I make a difference in the world?" and "How does my experience in the world unite me with others?"

Being intentional about figuring out who we are and the meaning of our lives in the context of the world around us is an honorable undertaking. In my mind, there couldn't be a more important time in history to embrace this work and to bring our spirits to the forefront.

Inevitably, when we face challenges in our personal lives such as a health crisis, the death of a loved one, the loss of a relationship, or financial misfortune, we are plunged into the abyss of the search for meaning. In the same way, when we are faced with a myriad of societal challenges such as racial injustice, political unrest, a global pandemic, and an economic crisis, we also find ourselves deeply questioning who we are and how we can make an impact on the world around us. We are being pummeled daily by a barrage of information through social media and other avenues that can be very distressing. It is paramount that we address this distress by caring for ourselves, and one of the ways we can do that is by embracing the journey this book offers. It is an excellent opportunity to nourish ourselves and grow.

I believe it is this inner personal work that will lead to the essential changes needed in our outer world and bring us together in our common humanness. Enjoy the journey ahead! May the experience be transformative for you and the world around you.

Priscilla Abercrombie, RN, NP, Ph.D

Frederic C. Craigie, Jr., Ph.D.

Introduction

In August, 2004, my friend and psychologist colleague Peter Flournoy, Ph.D., died of cancer at the age of 45.

Peter was a remarkable person, an energetic professional, and a gentle soul. He experienced his cancer as a blessing that taught him more about life than he otherwise would have understood. He packed a lot into the last couple of years of his life, ice climbing several times and sea kayaking to Monhegan Island (ten miles off the Maine coast—not for the faint of heart) a month before his death.

Peter was also excited about his spiritual life, which was informed particularly by Buddhist philosophy and practice in his last years. His memorial service took place on a glorious summer day. We who attended all received a card with a favorite meditative image of Peter's and his words:

> Life has taught me not to grasp and hold but to stand with a flat empty hand and allow the flow to happen. What is unfolding itself to me now is enough. By aligning myself with this energy, I remain amused, fed, and delighted by life. Deciding ahead what will make me happy and waiting that to manifest itself before I allow myself to experi-

ence happiness is missing the point. Happiness is in the seeing and the experiencing. Happiness is a simple thing; it comes from living life, rather than planning to live life. Life is not a rehearsal; it is what is happening *right now.*

By 2004, I had been professionally active in the arena of spirituality and health for many years. I published what I believe was the first article on spirituality in the Family Medicine literature in the mid-eighties and founded what is now the oldest nonsectarian academic symposium on spirituality and health in the United States in 1987. I did further research. I wrote grants. I started a department of spiritual care at our hospital. I developed curricula. I focused on healthcare and community applications of spirituality on sabbaticals. And I assembled a small interest group of colleagues at my home institution, the Maine-Dartmouth Family Medicine Residency, who would gather together periodically for dinner and conversation.

As a way of honoring Peter and passing along his wisdom, I decided to share his words with my interest group friends. I sent them all emails—I imagine it wasn't more than a dozen—and had some appreciative hallway conversations in the next couple of weeks. It occurred to me that it could be a good discipline for me and a good meditative opportunity for my friends to send out spiritually-informed quotations regularly. I distributed the famous comment, attributed in various translations to the French aviator and writer Antoine de Saint-Exupéry: "If you want to build a ship, don't drum up the men to gather wood, divide the work, and give orders. Instead, teach them to yearn for the vast and endless sea."

Fred's Reflections of the Week were off and running. More people asked to be included. I invited participants in my teaching and speaking engagements. I received emails from people who had heard of the reflections from their own friends and asked to be added to my distribution lists. As I write this, my weekly quotations/reflections—touching on spirituality, healing and well-being—go out to over 2000 people, and the file of accumulated quotations is over 40,000 words.

The *Fred's reflections* project is the genesis of this book. You have fifty-two from among hundreds and hundreds of quotations that I have sent out over the years. They come... both the larger list and this sample... from a remarkably diverse collection of authors. They represent science, the Arts, health care, business, journalism, academia, government, the recovery movement, and the arena of self-care and personal growth, in addition to more expressly spiritual fields. Together, these quotations provide rich perspectives on some of the essential questions that we all face:

- What does it mean to live a good life?
- What is sacred... what really matters?
- How do you address suffering and woundedness?
- Where do you find joy?
- Where is there hope in difficult circumstances?
- How can one person make a difference in the world?

These, and so many other questions that you can imagine and pose for yourself, mark the path (as the book subtitle suggests) of "meaningful, joyful, and peaceful living."

ABOUT THE BOOK

As you will see, the book is organized into 12 chapters, or thematic sections; Miracles, Aliveness, Purpose, Laughter and Joy, and eight others. I have organized these fairly randomly, and you will do well to pick up the book at any point to which your curiosity directs you.

Each meditation has four parts.

The first part presents a short, documented quotation. These quotations are rich in wisdom. Sometimes, I expect you will smile. Sometimes, you will nod knowingly. Often, I hope, you will find yourself curious about how the ideas presented in the quotations pertain to your life.

The second part of each meditation presents my own reflections. These arise from my professional and personal experience and from countless stories from other people, many of them first-hand or reliably second-hand. I can also point out that the reflections often have an empirical foundation. For several of the areas that we'll explore together—mindfulness, gratitude and forgiveness as examples—there are robust bodies of scientific research that have informed much of what I have to say. I have written enough scholarly material over the years—and I am not interested in layering this book with academic citations— that the foundation is there. If you are interested in exploring the empirical basis of some of these areas further, you can pursue the names and source citations that I give you or just go to our friends, Google Scholar or PubMed. On PubMed today, for instance, the search term "forgiveness" gets you over a thousand citations.

The third part of each meditation gives you questions for your own reflection and suggestions for how you might specifically follow up on each meditation during the week. What is your life experience with these ideas? What is your wisdom; what do *you* know about these ideas? How might you build on these reflections in your awareness and in your own exploration in the coming week?

The final section gives you biographical information about the authors of the quotations. I have found that learning some of the life stories of the people that I quote adds color, richness, and context to their ideas. For some authors who are not widely known, the entries are brief. For some other authors—the final meditation about Dorothy Day as an example—you'll have to pardon me for truncating long and complicated life stories.

A lot of thought went into the choice of a weekly format, by the way. There are many, many resources for daily study out there—the words *devotionals* or *disciplines* are often used—but not many on a weekly cycle. While a daily format is certainly useful for many people, I also think that the rhythm of modern life follows weekly cycles. Piano lessons are weekly. Therapy is weekly. My Fitbit organizes activity and health goals week-by-week. I hope that a weekly format will allow you to focus a little more intensively on each meditation and to explore key ideas with the reflections and suggested exercises over the course of several days.

I also want to say a few words about spirituality. You know that this has been an area of professional passion and expertise for me for many years. That said, you will find very little expressly spiritual or religious language in this book. It is very important for me to be inclusive, to welcome and speak to readers from different spiritual and religious traditions and to readers who follow no particular traditions, who form and follow their own personal and unique spiritual lives. I want to honor your own spiritual path, however you frame that, and to invite you to bring your own understanding of spirituality to the ideas and issues that we will be exploring together.

My understanding of spirituality, as it pertains to and transcends different traditions, has to do with what people experience as sacred. The questions that frame anyone's understanding of The Sacred, like those above, are spiritual questions. Who are you? What do you cherish? What do you love? What kind of person do you aspire to be? What keeps you going in hard times?

For most people, moreover, The Sacred is understood in and often rooted in their experience of God. "God," of course, goes by many names. Yahweh. Allah. Great Spirit. The Universe. Higher Power, or Higher Consciousness. More than one patient has referred to God, not entirely jokingly, I think, as "The Man Upstairs." With countless variations in language and image, most people hold beliefs about an overarching Presence... Spirit... Energy... that is often the basis of creation stories and stands to provide coherence, direction and comfort.

My own experience of God has been vital in my life. My understanding of God has evolved over the years, but I have always been particularly drawn to the idea, traditionally attributed to John the Evangelist in the Christian tradition, that God is love. Perhaps this may resonate also with readers whose spirituality is framed more in terms of a sacred Path than in terms of Divine relationships.

Your spirituality is your own, and I want to honor whatever ways you conceive of these eternal issues. Even without expressly spiritual language, though, I think of this as a deeply spiritual book, and I hope you may experience it that way, as well.

About Me

I am a clinical psychologist and medical educator. Before launching into what I call "semi-retirement," I was a faculty member for over 35 years at a family medicine residency in central Maine. My educational role was teaching residents and medical students about behavioral health issues and helping them to value and cultivate their own resilience and well-being. My clinical role was providing behavioral health care in our outpatient primary care practice, working with a largely underserved population. Since 2004, I have also been a faculty member at the Andrew Weil Center for Integrative Medicine (it has gone by other names in earlier years) at the University of Arizona College of Medicine, where I coordinate curricula in spirituality and healing relationships. And you know some additional details about my work with spirituality and health.

That's some of the professional information. I also want to tell you a little about who I am, and who I am not, at a more personal level. Readers, I believe, deserve this.

I am a scientist. I am an observer and a collector of stories. As a teacher, I am privileged, as all teachers are, to be able to learn from students. As a clinician, I am privileged, as all clinicians are, to be able to learn from those people we variously call "clients," or "patients," or—I like this best—"fellow travelers." I am, like you, on a journey.

If you're looking for people who have personal odysseys of suffering and overcoming suffering, it's not me. Like anybody, I have had a few rough patches, but overall, it's been a comfortable and undramatic life. My parents loved me. I went to a great public high school, an old and prestigious college, and a good graduate school (which was, by the way, in the era of generous National Institute of Mental Health traineeships, largely free). I have been singularly blessed to have been married to a wonderful woman since 1973. My three children and their partners are remarkable people. I have six incredible grandchildren and a loving extended family. My life, as I write this, allows ample time to spend with all of them, along with opportunities to be professionally active pretty much on my own terms. I'm not in the one percent, but neither do I worry about where the next meal is coming from or whether there will continue to be a roof over my head. With allowance for the fact that the joints aren't quite what they used to be, I'm a healthy and active guy.

Demographics are pertinent, too. I am an Anglo white male. If you are a woman, or someone with an ethnic or cultural minority background, or someone from the LG-BTQ community, I am thrilled and honored to have you here, but I can't pretend to understand the nuances of your life experience.

I have tried to listen carefully to people over the years who have had different experiences and backgrounds, but it's a project of continuing learning and one that I take seriously. If some of what I say doesn't resonate with your life experience, please know that it's not because I don't care or that I think I have a corner on the market for wisdom.

I hope you will feel a spirit of humility in how I present the ideas in this book to you. I want to share with you some of the experiences and ideas that have marked the path for me, but just as much, I hope this book invites and empowers your own ideas about what it means to live a good life.

USING THE BOOK

I have designed this book with the thought that it can be particularly meaningful as you are actively engaged with the material. Below are three suggestions for using this book.

First, spend some time with my questions for reflection. As I have said, these are prompts to think about how the ideas pertain to your life in the past, in the present, and in the future.

Second, do the exercises. For each meditation, there is a recommendation of specific activities you can pursue during the week. I think you will find that exploring the ways that the ideas from each meditation fit into your everyday life will add depth, and perhaps some new insights, to your experience.

Third, consider working with this material with someone else. You can certainly make your way along with the book individually, but sharing this with other people holds special advantages. You learn from hearing other people's experiences, and you learn by forming and giving voice to your own ideas and putting them out there. You might pair up with one other person—a partner, a neighbor or friend, a sibling—or you might find that the book is well-suited for group study in your personal circle or in your community.

Welcome, and thank you for coming along on this adventure. May you find some new insights, some challenges, some substantial affirmation, and continuing growth on your journey.

Fred
Tucson, Arizona
May, 2020

Frederic C. Craigie, Jr., Ph.D.

MIRACLES

Frederic C. Craigie, Jr., Ph.D.

1

There are only two ways to live your life. One is as though nothing is a miracle. The other is as though everything is.

Albert Einstein/Gilbert Fowler White

A young woman hobbles to the shrine at Lourdes, throws away her crutches, and walks. A middle-aged man is diagnosed with inoperable liver cancer and six months later, it's gone. A 5-month-old baby is discovered alive in the rubble of an earthquake in Nepal, having survived against all odds for nearly a day. Nineteen golfers in Colorado suffer a direct lightning strike and live.

In our culture, we think about miracles in events like these; potentially-dire situations that turn out in ways that far exceed reasonable expectations or rational explanations. Sometimes, we embrace them; sometimes, we are skeptical. Almost always, they are cause for celebration.

But spiritually, the idea of miracles runs deeper. *Everything* is a miracle.

Word origins are often revealing. Our modern word *miracle* has its roots in the Latin *miraculum/mirari/mirus;*

referring to an "object of wonder," a "marvel," and inspiring "awe and admiration." The Latin, in turn, has origins in the earlier *smeiros/sméyros,* to "smile or laugh."

With this broader understanding, miracles are not so much mysterious deviations from what we think is possible. Rather, they are things that are all around us, that we hold in wonder and awe, and that make us smile.

You cut your finger chopping kale. You clean it up and do the usual first aid care, and a week later, there is absolutely no indication at all that anything happened to your finger.

Your infant daughter crawls one day and joyfully takes halting steps the next. Your infant daughter grows up, and you smile as you see her marry a person that she loves.

A letter travels across the country with such accuracy that neither you nor anyone you know has ever experienced a postal error. A military cargo plane with a takeoff weight of almost 175 tons flies. Somehow, there is enough water for millions of people in Tucson and Phoenix, the principal populated areas of the Sonoran Desert, where I live seasonally. With scattered clouds on a summer day, the sunset lights up the sky with vibrant shades of red and orange. You are alive, and you have the ability to choose the kind of person you want to be as you live your life.

Are these not "objects of wonder?" Do they (some of them—you might have your doubts about the postal service and you might not think much about cargo planes) make you smile? Are they not miracles?

Reflection

- What difference might it make for you if you were to view *everything* as a miracle?

- What has there been in your everyday life this week that has been "an object of wonder" and has made you smile?

Author

Albert Einstein (1879-1955) was a world-renowned physicist who profoundly changed our understanding of time and space. It is noteworthy for this particular reflection that four of his seminal papers were produced in one year, 1905, which has been described as his *annus mirabilis* (miracle year).

The provenance of this familiar quotation is not clear. I find no direct record of Einstein having said it although he did write often about the relationship of science and his spiritual views. He did famously say, "The most beautiful emotion we can experience is the mystical. It is the power of all true art and science. He to whom this emotion is a stranger, who can no longer wonder and stand rapt in awe, is as good as dead. To know that what is impenetrable to us really exists, manifesting itself as the highest wisdom and the most radiant beauty, which our dull faculties can comprehend only in their most primitive forms—this knowledge, this feeling, is at the center of true religiousness."

The "miracles" quotation was documented (attributing it to Einstein) in the 1940s by **Gilbert Fowler White (1911-2006).** White was an American geographer with special interests in flooding and water management. Active in the Society of Friends, he was a conscientious objector in World War II, working with refugees in France. He was also a distinguished academic, serving for several years as president of Haverford College and teaching at the University of Chicago and University of Colorado. His *New York Times* obituary comments that his "philosophy of accommodating nature instead of trying to master it had profound effects on policy and environmental thought."

2

Miracles… seem to me to rest not so much upon faces or voices or healing power coming suddenly near to us from afar off but upon our own perception being made finer, so that for a moment our eyes can see and our ears can hear what is there about us always.

Willa Cather

To behold the wondrous miracles of everyday life you have to see.

Consider the miracle of moveable wall sections. For tens of thousands of years of human history, people created dwelling structures with portals for coming and going. They covered these portals with weavings or bear hides, which gave them some visual privacy and cut down the wind and cold, but were not particularly helpful in securing their homes against intruding animals or marauding neighbors. Then, somewhere, someone invented the hinge. With the hinge, everything changed. People could now make their portals into doorways when they wished to come and go and make their portals into walls when they wanted security. An object of wonder, indeed.

Frederic C. Craigie, Jr., Ph.D.

I'm sure you can find countless examples in the built environment and in the natural world, things that complete the sentence, "When you really think about it, isn't it incredible that…" Last summer, I had FaceTime calls with my Oregon family from the UK, 4600 miles away, instantaneous, rich in sound, and visual clarity. Skyscrapers are now 2000 feet tall. People have flown to the moon. Flocks of birds somehow know to make instantaneous turns together. Forests regenerate after devastating fires. People are endowed with emotions that give them vital information about how to navigate through the world.

It is in our ability to pause, to really see these things that are "about us always," that the ordinary becomes miraculous.

How is it that our perception may be made finer? It is a practice, a discipline. A spiritual practice. Stopping to examine everything that we tend to take for granted wouldn't leave much time for living our lives, but a practice of pausing, sometimes, to really see and hear opens our hearts to the wonder that is all around.

The spiritual practice of pausing can be intentional. As you read this, pause to look around. Perhaps, think back over your experiences in the last day or two. What do you notice that makes you smile in wonder?

Or, the spiritual practice of pausing can mean choosing to sit with the wonder in something that comes to you as a surprise. Putting together Legos with children (a universal experience among the parents and grandparents whom I know), it occurred to me that it is miraculous how the company creates these little blocks with such precise tolerances that they are easy for little hands to put together and pull apart, yet hold securely once attached. This makes me smile, too.

Reflection

- Pause once or twice a day to really see something ordinary and allow the miracle—the object of wonder—to appear.

- Do this for a few days. What do you notice about your sense of wonder? What difference does this make for you?

Author

Willa Cather (1873-1947) was an American writer, poet and editor, who is best known for her novels of the West in the early years of European settlement. She was born in Virginia and moved with her family to the Nebraska frontier in 1883, being amazed and unsettled by the vast and barren landscape she encountered. As she began to write, her career took her to New York where she served for several years as managing editor of *McClure's Magazine*, whose authors included Joseph Conrad and Henry James. The third volume of her Prairie Trilogy, *One of Ours*, was awarded the Pulitzer Prize in 1922.

The quotation comes from her 1927 novel, *Death Comes for the Archbishop*, the story of a young Catholic bishop who is called to establish a diocese in the newly-formed territory of New Mexico. It is spoken by the bishop to his friend Joseph. The complete quotation is that "Miracles *of the Church* seem to me to rest..." This detail is appropriate to the novel, but it seems to me that the idea is not limited to the Christian tradition, and I have presented it in the form in which it is commonly cited.

Frederic C. Craigie, Jr., Ph.D.

–𝕭–

The further I wake into this life, the more I realize that Love is everywhere and the extraordinary is waiting quietly beneath the skin of all that is ordinary. Light is in both the broken bottle and the diamond, and music is in both the flowing violin and the water dripping from the drainage pipe. Yes, Love is under the porch as well as on the top of the mountain, and joy is both in the front row and in the bleachers, if we are willing to be where we are.

Mark Nepo

It's always a delight to see family greetings in airports. When I travel, or when I'm waiting for arriving visitors, I pause to watch the little celebrations. Couples come back together. Little children run to grandparents, who toss them into the air. Families hold banners; "Welcome home, Trevor and Kate!"

We can certainly appreciate miracles—objects of wonder—in the physical world. People flying to the moon, doors that open and close, crocuses popping through the snow in the spring. But isn't it the greatest miracle that you are loved? And isn't it the greatest miracle that you can love?

Love is everywhere.

Love is in the sentinel events of your life. The birth of a child. Marriage. The mixture of grief and celebration at the passing of someone who has been dear to you.

Love is also in the countless joys of daily life. An elderly couple walks hand in hand. A kindergarten teacher gets down on the level of a little girl and really listens. A golden retriever wags his whole body when his owner comes down the stairs in the morning, and his owner is just as enthralled to see him.

In working with many people around family relationships over the years, I've commented that it is easy to love somebody when they are cheerful and engaging. The real challenge is how not to lose sight of love when someone is not.

I saw a man who had been married for many years to a woman who had significant, episodic emotional difficulties. She could be sweet one day and caustic and isolated the next. "It's not easy," he said, "but I try to be kind when she's like that. I know her behavior isn't who she really is, and I know that when she gets upset, kindness will usually help her to feel a little more peaceful. Even in the ugliness of life," he continued, "you can't let the ugliness keep you from the joy and the beauty."

Love, the object of wonder. The miracle.

Reflection

- Think about a time when you have been loved, a time, perhaps, when you were not especially easy to love. Do you see the miracle?

- Open your heart to continuing ways, and to new ways, that you can express the miracle of love in the coming week.

Author

Mark Nepo (b. 1951) is a poet and philosopher, the author of over a dozen books and audiotapes, including the acclaimed collection of daily reflections, *The Book of Awakening* (Conari, 2011), from which the quotation comes. A survivor of cancer in his thirties, Nepo highlights the transformational journey toward full, present, and joyful living even in the presence of suffering.

Frederic C. Craigie, Jr., Ph.D.

–4–

*Although the world is full of suffering,
it is also full of the overcoming of it.*

Helen Keller

The story of the man being kind to his challenged wife introduces a vital element in the idea of miracles. Thinking of miracles as "objects of wonder," calling forth "awe and admiration," making you smile... does not presume a rosy and gleeful understanding of life.

To the contrary. Life entails suffering, and it is perhaps in the setting of suffering that the ability to pause and behold at least the shadow of the miracle can be most life-giving.

As we move toward the end of the second decade of this century, the cohort of women and men who survived the Holocaust is dwindling, but their powerful stories remain. Edith Herz was born in 1926 to a comfortable Jewish family in Germany. They lived in Worms, which had been a center of Jewish culture for hundreds of years. Her parents operated a small and successful business, and their extended family enjoyed the same opportunities of community life, travel, and spiritual practice as other Europeans of the time.

With the rise of the Nazi movement, this began to change. The coordinated attacks on the Jewish community of *Kristallnacht*—the Night of Shattered Glass in November, 1938—witnessed the desecration of over a thousand synagogues, the destruction of several thousand Jewish businesses, and the internment of 30,000 Jews. Edith's father, a decorated German veteran of the Great War, her mother, and Edith were transported to Thereseinstadt, which was a labor camp and holding area for Jews who were later moved to death camps to the east. Edith's father died there, and in the following months, Edith and her mother were sent to Birkenau/Auschwitz, where it is estimated that over a million people perished, and subsequently to Stutthof concentration camp, from which they were liberated by the Russian army in January 1945. In addition to Edith's father, 16 uncles, aunts, and cousins had been killed.

Edith uses the word *miracle* to describe a number of remarkable events that allowed her and her mother to survive. With dozens of other women, they are herded into the gas chamber, and it malfunctions. She is called before Josef Mengele, and he waves her to the right, to labor, rather than to the left, to death. A German officer on Christmas break offers her a morsel of food.

More broadly, she credits her survival to her partnership with a remarkable mother and to their shared spirit of "hope" and "optimism." "What good would it do," she asks, "to whine and cry? None. Those who did, perished." She and her mother maintained a sacred commitment to be together, supporting one another in the inevitable times when one of them felt like giving up.

Weekly Soul

The world is full of suffering and of the overcoming of it. Is this not a miracle?

Reflection

- Think of a time when you have made your way past suffering. How did this happen? Do you see some miracle, some object of wonder?

- Notice how you address times of challenge or disappointment in the coming week. What, indeed, would the miracle look like... how would you want to be addressing times of challenge or disappointment?

Author

Helen Keller (1880-1968) is surely legendary in her overcoming the suffering of deafness and blindness with the support of her teacher, Anne Sullivan. Appropriate to our subject, the theatrical and film rendition of the relationship of Sullivan with Keller was called *The Miracle Worker*.

Keller graduated from Radcliffe College in 1904, the first deaf/blind person to earn a bachelor's degree. Her adult life consisted of advocacy for causes related to disabilities and widespread political activity, helping to found the American Civil Liberties Union, and speaking on behalf of women's suffrage, socialist causes, and international peacemaking.

The quotation comes from Keller's 1903 book, *Optimism*. Readers might appreciate the larger context:

> I know what evil is. Once or twice I have wrestled with it, and for a time felt its chilling touch on my life; so, I speak with knowledge when I say that evil is of no consequence, except as a sort

of mental gymnastic. For the very reason that I have come in contact with it, I am more truly an optimist. I can say with conviction that the struggle which evil necessitates is one of the greatest blessings. It makes us strong, patient, helpful men and women. It lets us into the soul of things and teaches us that although the world is full of suffering, it is full also of the overcoming of it. My optimism, then, does not rest on the absence of evil but on a glad belief in the preponderance of good and a willing effort always to cooperate with the good, that it may prevail. I try to increase the power God has given me to see the best in everything and everyone, and make that Best a part of my life. The world is sown with good; but unless I turn my glad thoughts into practical living and till my own field, I cannot reap a kernel of the good.

Edith Pagelson (b. 1926) eventually came to America and has been blessed in relationships with two husbands who have passed on. She aims to strike a balance between remembering and speaking about the Holocaust and living a full current life. Her story, written in collaboration with my colleague and friend Ronnie Weston, is available in *Against All Odds: A Miracle of Holocaust Survival* (Rockland, Maine: Maine Authors Publishing, 2012).

ALIVENESS

Frederic C. Craigie, Jr., Ph.D.

–5–

Don't ask what the world needs; ask what makes you come alive, and go do it. Because what the world needs is people who have come alive.

Howard Thurman

Several years ago, I was in Chicago for a professional conference. Life-long baseball player, fan, and addict that I am, I never pass up an opportunity to see a major league game on the road. I took the Red Line to the Sox-35th Avenue stop for U. S. Cellular Field (where the White Sox play; it will always be "Comisky Park" to me) and got off with the crowd.

On the platform was a small, thin, elderly man with Chinese features, playing a two-stringed fiddle (which I later learned is called an erhu) with the accompaniment of a small CD player. The music had a beat to it and was really moving along. His eyes were closed, as in reverie, and he had a smile on his lips.

Facing him was a young African American woman dancing to the music. Enthralled, arms and legs flowing with the music, her face an image of delight. It was clear to me that they hadn't come together as an act; it was more that they were drawn together—crossing divides of age and culture—by the energy of the music. The crowd mostly shuffled past, heading to the game. A few people paused. I was captivated by how alive they both were in that special moment together.

Most of us want to save the world. Sometimes, we aim to change the world through social and community activism—volunteering at the food bank, serving on a nonprofit board, marching for a cause, teaching English to refugees. Sometimes, we find life and aliveness in ventures like these.

But do we not also bring a little goodness into the world just by the very experience of being fully alive? The musicians at the subway stop were not, I assume, driven by an assessment of "what the world needs." They were immersed in their passions for music—alive to their passions for music—and the energy of that moment touched the heart, at least, of a middle-aged psychologist walking by.

There are four reasons to cultivate and give expression to "what makes you come alive."

- It's good for your soul, and probably, for your body. You add to your ledger of resilience and wholeness with an accumulation of moments when you are enthralled with your life.

- Aliveness creates energy that ripples out into the world. You know this; you have felt touched in the same way that I have when you have been in the presence of someone who was fully alive.

- Your particular contributions to the world—your vocation, your career, how you choose to spend your time—will be more genuine and impactful if they "make you come alive." I have worked with physicians and other health care providers whose hearts were not in their work, and I have known others who clearly found deep delight and joy in their work even amid the daily frustrations and challenges that we all face. I can tell you whom I will seek out for care when the need comes.

- What are you doing with your life, anyway, if not to live in full and vital ways?

If you do noble things to save the world that are outside the circle of your heart, it draws the life out of you and doesn't really change anything. If you nurture the things that make you come alive, you are indeed addressing what the world needs.

Alas, the game, by the way, was rained out.

Reflection

- Think of a time when you have felt fully alive. Recall a story.

- When have you become so engaged with something that you have lost track of time?

- The flip side... when have you felt spiritually and emotionally dead? What do you stand to learn from this?

- How would you rate your aliveness on a scale of 0-10? What might you do to move up one level?

Author

The Rev. Dr. Howard Thurman (1899-1981) was an African-American theologian, educator, writer and civil rights activist. Born into poverty, he was raised by a grandmother who was a former slave. He pursued an education at Morehouse College and Rochester Theological Semi-

nary and subsequently served as a pastor, seminary professor and dean at Howard University, Founder (with the
Fellowship of Reconciliation) of first racially integrated,
intercultural church in the United States, the Church for
the Fellowship of All Peoples in San Francisco, and then
professor and dean and Boston University.

Thurman was at the forefront of social thought and
issues of justice and reconciliation in the mid-twentieth
century. He studied with the Quaker mystic Rufus Jones in
the late twenties, and then, in 1935-36, participated in the
first African-American Delegation of Friendship to India
and adjoining countries. It was on this trip that Thurman
and two colleagues met with Mohandas Gandhi, and were
moved by Gandhi's ideas about social change and intercultural understanding. Thurman's writing, in turn, was
strongly influential for Martin Luther King, Jr., and other
leaders of the American civil rights movement.

–❻–

Although the spiritual dimension is always present, people are not aware of it. If we think of this in terms of images, we can say we have a vintage wine cellar, but we rarely drink from it. We have an interior castle, and we seldom visit it. There is a treasure buried in our field, and we do not know how to unearth it... The distinction between the presence of the spiritual and the awareness of the spiritual is foundational in spiritual teaching and sets in motion the spiritual project. We are asleep, and we need to awake; we are blind, and we need to see; we are deaf, and we need to hear; we are lost, and we need to be found; we are dead and we need to come back to life. All these images point to the spiritual venture of becoming aware of what is there.

Jack Shea

You are alive as you are aware of what is there.

The experience of aliveness is rooted in the life of the spirit. When you partake of the vintage wine cellar, when you visit the interior castle, when you unearth the buried treasure… when you experience the richness that is always there… you are alive.

C. Everett Koop, M.D., was a pioneering pediatric surgeon and Surgeon General during the Reagan administration. He is best noted for his campaign against smoking and for his insistence that the government not turn a blind eye on the incipient HIV/AIDS crisis. He was also a deeply spiritual man. Our appointments together in the same Department of Family and Community Medicine at Dartmouth Medical School privileged me to invite him to be the keynote presenter in 1994 at an annual symposium on spirituality and health that I had founded in 1987. Memorably, his definition of "spirituality" was "the vital center of a person; that which is held sacred."

Our modern words, *vital* and *vitality* come from the Latin *vitalis*, which means pertaining to "life" or "life force." The spiritual life—the experience of vitality—has to do with being aware of the sacredness that is there, waiting to be explored and expressed.

Aliveness, as Thurman points out, follows behavior. Do what makes you come alive. But aliveness also follows from attitudes and perspectives and awareness.

Think of some of the most ordinary and banal moments in your daily life: carting groceries from the store back to the car, brushing your teeth, paying the light bill, and taking out the trash. Is there not something sacred undergirding these moments?

You are alive. You breathe. You move. You are capable of experiencing emotions. You can form words and express ideas. You can love and be loved. You can suffer, and you can find and chart paths to resilience and growth. You can live your own, completely unique, irreplaceable life.

You can't, of course, reflect on these things to the exclusion of doing what you need to do. You have to drive home, unpack the groceries, and make dinner. But might you pause, sometimes, to partake of the flow of aliveness and vitality by opening your heart to what is there?

And don't linger too long in the wine cellar.

Reflection

- Pause, sometime, in a particularly ordinary moment in your daily life. Use all of your senses to experience this moment.

- Reflect on the sacredness that undergirds this moment. What is there that you cherish about your life that is part of the flow of this moment?

- Open yourself to the energy of being truly alive, even in this ordinary moment. What difference might this make for you as you carry this forward?

Author

John (Jack) Shea, STD, is a theologian, master storyteller, and poet whose long-time passion has been supporting the spiritual formation and life of individuals and groups. Among a number of positions along the way, he previously served as Professor of Systematic Theology and Director of the Doctor of Ministry Program at the University of St. Mary of the Lake. The author of over two dozen books, he lectures and consults widely to faith-based organizations about theological reflection and formation, and values-based corporate life. You can read more about his work at www.jackshea.org.

I met Jack when he graciously invited me in 1999 to take part in a colloquium, sponsored by the Park Ridge Center for the Study of Health, Faith, and Ethics, exploring practical approaches to incorporating spirituality in health care. The quotation comes from *Spirituality and Health care: Reaching toward a Holistic Future* (The Park Ridge Center, 2000), which grew out of the proceedings of that colloquium.

– 7 –

People say that what we're all seeking is meaning for life. I don't think that's what we're really seeking. I think that what we're seeking is an experience of being alive so that our life experiences on a purely physical plane will have resonances within our innermost being and reality, so that we actually feel the rapture of being alive.

Joseph Campbell

You are alive as you live your own life.

There are so many forces that draw us to live other people's lives. We live in a culture that relentlessly champions the external trappings of success. Newer cars are better than older. Bigger houses are better than smaller. Higher salaries are better than lower. Being one of the vice presidents of your company is better than being among the line staff. Being young and sleek is better than being older and heavy. There is nothing inherently wrong with such things, but ultimately, they are false gods, poor places to hang your hat for your emotional and spiritual life. You are alive as you give expression to your own innermost being.

For that matter, choices that you make that run counter to our "bigger and better" cultural values—training as a social worker to work in prisons, buying a used Prius rather than a mega F-350—will ultimately ring hollow if they move you to lead somebody else's life, rather than your own. Aliveness starts on the inside.

In 2004, psychologists Christopher Peterson and Martin Seligman published a momentous compendium that summarized several years' work exploring human character. *Character Strengths and Virtues* (published jointly by Oxford University Press and the American Psychological Association) arose from anthropological research and an exhaustive examination of writing, from Plato and Aristotle to Hallmark greeting cards, about what it means to live a good life. The resulting framework identifies six "virtues" that are universally esteemed across time and culture (wisdom, courage, humanity, justice, temperance and transcendence), and 24 "strengths of character" (such as curiosity, perseverance, kindness, humility, and appreciation of beauty) that are "pathways" that enable people to give expression to these virtues. This work provides the foundation for the modern Positive Psychology movement. You can explore this further at www.viacharacter.org/.

Follow up research has looked at relationships among these elements in fine detail, but the basic premise remains the same. You are hard-wired to have one or more of these character strengths resonate prominently in your life, and your expression of your particular strengths of character is closely associated with your life satisfaction, happiness and well-being. If kindness is a signature strength for you, then your well-being will be enhanced by being kind. If fairness is a signature strength for you then your well-being will be enhanced by treating people fairly. If humor is a signature strength for you then your well-being will be enhanced by making other people smile or laugh. And so forth.

Aliveness, then, has to do with the ways in which your activities and relationships are formed by the personal qualities and values that are vital to you. Your "innermost being."

This is good news for living in an imperfect and challenging world. Even in the midst of uninspiring or challenging times there is a flow of life... of aliveness... in tuning in to the inner qualities and values that are vital and sacred for you.

I see this all the time. Working with hundreds of physicians, I can't count the times I have heard, "There are so many things that can bring me down... documentation, electronic health records, productivity requirements... but when I close the door and work with a patient, I get recharged. I remember that this is why I'm a doctor." So it is with me, also. I dutifully attend committee meetings and write grant applications, but when I meet with someone and help them in some small way to feel more empowered to be who they really are, it can be exhilarating.

I *do* think that we're seeking meaning in life by the way, but the idea that aliveness follows the expression of our "innermost being" is right on.

Reflection

- How would you put into words what "innermost being" means to you?

- Think of times... think of stories... when you have expressed these inner qualities. What has this been like for you?

- Take the VIA ("Values in Action") survey that is linked to the website above. You have to register, but it's free. How do the results about your signature strengths of character expand your understanding of your "innermost being?"

Author

Joseph Campbell (1904–1987) was an American academic and writer best known for his seminal work on the origins, nature, and functions of myth. He began his college studies at Dartmouth, transferring to Columbia, where he received bachelor's and master's degrees in literature. Not seeing eye-to-eye with Columbia faculty about doctoral studies, he embarked on a life-long program of intensive self-study through reading, world-wide travel, and collaboration with a host of 20th century luminaries, including John Steinbeck, Jiddu Krishnamurti, and, more recently, George Lucas and Bill Moyers. Campbell's principal teaching engagement was a 38-year tenure at Sarah Lawrence College. The quotation is from an interview with Bill Moyers that was part of a PBS series, *The Power of Myth*, which was aired after Campbell's death and subsequently published in book form.

–8–

Irenaeus, the great early church father, said the glory of God is a human being fully alive. Now, if you back off from every little controversy in your life, you're not alive, and what's more, you're boring. It's a terrible thing that we settle for so much less... The greatest pleasure for me was being with black civil rights leaders and followers, because they were so alive. You can be more alive in pain than in complacency. These often very poor blacks in Alabama, Mississippi, and Georgia, were so wonderfully alive, so cheerful, so courageous.

William Sloane Coffin

You are alive as you extend yourself on behalf of something that matters.

William Sloane Coffin was no stranger to controversy. He certainly could have led, in his words, a "polite" and "comfortable" life as a clergyman and college chaplain, but in addition to these ministries, he was immersed over many years in activism on behalf of justice and peace—civil rights, gay rights, nuclear disarmament, antiwar advocacy—that brought him into conflict with the established order.

His example of aliveness comes from his participation in Freedom Rides of the 1960; African American people in the Deep South who came together in the vilified and perilous work toward equality.

There is aliveness in the commitment to a cause that matters to you.

When my wife and I moved to our home in a pleasant neighborhood in a small college town in Maine a number of years ago, the historic 1913 high school building a couple of blocks away was in its waning days. It was finally abandoned and became, in the words of a city official, "a magnet for vandalism and squatters." After several failed attempts to convert the building into something else or even tear it down (apparently prohibitively expensive for public buildings of that vintage), developers appeared who had particular expertise in renovating historic properties for beneficial community purposes. They presented a plan to convert the building into affordable housing while maintaining the design features of the building that gave it its unique character.

Months of planning meetings for public input followed, along with town council meetings at which key decisions were made at successive stages of the project's evolution.

Early on, the fault lines became clear. There was a large and vocal contingent of neighbors from our part of the community who were adamantly opposed to the project. You may anticipate their concerns. Lower income people would be a blight on the neighborhood. Property values would go down. Traffic would increase. With one other person who made a token appearance, my wife and I were the only public supporters of the project. We thought that affordable housing was vitally important to our community, that diversity increases rather than decreases the richness of community life, and that the developer had had a strong track record of planning and subsequently managing such renovations in a successful way.

We were not popular. I recall vividly the scene of sitting in a town council meeting, alone with the primary developer in an otherwise vacant half of the room, with the other half of the room filled with doubtful and visibly unsettled neighbors. I recall comments to the council from nay-sayers being greeted with enthusiastic applause and with my comments to the council being met with icy silence. I recall angry and critical interchanges in the hallway and nasty emails.

Looking back, my personal experience was a mixture of loneliness and exhilaration. It was uncomfortable, and yet even in the face of criticism and disdain, I felt a sense of aliveness, that I was standing up for something that mattered to me and to the larger well-being of my community.

The project was completed, by the way, and remains a vital community resource and a peaceful and attractive element of the neighborhood. The first people who moved in were two retired nuns.

In these stories, there are degrees of perilousness. My experience was unpleasant, but I wasn't going to be arrested, beaten up, or, heaven forbid, shot or lynched as were some of our African American sisters and brothers.

But aliveness in extending yourself on behalf of something that matters does not necessarily depend on degree of peril. You are alive when you make a comment that runs counter to the flow of a conversation, when it would be easier to stay silent. You are alive when you raise an idea that stands to move people in new and uncertain directions. You are alive when you join a community of people who are working together to redress an injustice. What you say or do doesn't have to be perfect, eloquent, or even successful. It just has to come from the heart.

Reflection

- Think of a time when you said or did something that arose from your own values even if you knew it might run counter to someone else's thinking. What was this like for you?

- Reflect particularly on the idea of "extending yourself," going beyond the place where you would feel completely comfortable and safe.

- Notice, in the week to come, opportunities to say or do something that comes from the heart, when it would be easier to hold off.

Author

William Sloane Coffin (1924-2006) was an American clergyman and social activist. He grew up in a wealthy New York family with a long tradition of engagement with progressive and charitable causes. His initial passion was music, and he studied piano with renowned teachers in Europe, intending on a career as a concert pianist. With the onset of the Second World War, Coffin enlisted in the army and was involved with military intelligence, subsequently continuing this work with the CIA in its efforts to counteract Soviet influence in Europe. He left this career as he became disillusioned with the CIA role in the overthrow of the democratically-elected president of Guatemala, who had run afoul of American interests with policies of agrarian reform benefitting hundreds of thousands of indigenous people. He graduated from Yale Divinity School and served as chaplain at Williams College and at Yale and later as pastor of the Riverside Church in New York. He is best remembered for his outspoken advocacy and leadership in issues of peace and civil rights, collaborating with Martin Luther King, Desmond Tutu, Nelson Mandela and others, but he found particular joy in individual pastoral work with young people. The quotation comes from an interview, two years before his death, with journalist Bob Abernethy on the PBS program, *Religion and Ethics Newsweekly.*

Frederic C. Craigie, Jr., Ph.D.

–❾–

*All changes are a risk… but change makes you know
that you're alive. You're exploring, you're stumbling–
almost certainly stumbling if my past is any indication–
but there is a certain exhilaration, too. You can't wait to
see what happens next… What I like most about change
is that it's a synonym for "hope." If you are taking a risk,
what you are really saying is, "I believe in tomorrow,
and I will be a part of it."*

Linda Ellerbee

You are alive as you extend yourself on behalf of something new.

Advocating for ideas and causes is one type of risk,
but the experience of aliveness in risk and change is much
broader than that. You are alive as you venture out of your
accustomed and comfortable ways of being—we use the
modern phrase, *comfort zone*—to take up something that
you haven't done before that expands a little bit the scope
of who you are.

There are big ways of doing this, like the archetypal
story of the investment broker who forsakes the corner of-

fice on the 33rd floor in New York to move to Colorado to herd cattle. (People really do come from the Big City to Maine, I should say, with stories like this, seeking a more peaceful off-the-grid life.)

Henri Nouwen was a Dutch Catholic priest and theologian who held prestigious appointments teaching at Yale and Harvard Divinity Schools and was the author of over 40 books of spiritual commentary and reflection. His academic life gave him opportunities to explore very different communities, spending several months at a Trappist monastery in upstate New York and later accepting the invitation of a friend to visit the L'Arche community—providing homes and services for people with intellectual disabilities—in France. Nouwen was so touched by the service and spirit of mutuality in being in community with people at L'Arche that he eventually made his way to the L'Arche community in Ontario, where he remained for the rest of his life. His relationships there provided him with a sense of aliveness—his phrase was "at-homeness"—that he had not experienced in his more conventional and prominent public life.

Perhaps you have had some similar experience of a big life change—taking a different job, moving to a different community, or choosing a life partner. But is there not aliveness in the smaller, day-to-day ways that we all take on some risk to extend ourselves beyond our up-to-that-point definition of who we are?

One of my students recently told the story that she had led a sedate and bookish life growing up and had never been especially interested in athletics or outdoor activities until her new husband "got me into running." She started slowly but quickly found that she was becoming "hooked," working up to the point where she completed a half-marathon. "I never would have guessed," she says, "but running gives me a real sense of accomplishment and, actually, joy."

I can think of countless other examples:

- learning a new language and haltingly talking with a native speaker;
- doing something on a public stage: speaking, singing, reading poetry;
- trying out a new recipe when Chris and Barbara come over for dinner;
- finally, after all these years, taking piano lessons;
- painting the kitchen cabinets a new and vibrant color;
- trading in your Ford Taurus for a little spiffier vehicle for your commute;
- setting the alarm to get up at 3 AM to see the lunar eclipse;

and

- getting down to eye level with a little child and really listening;
- having coffee with someone who is at a different place in their political views; and/or
- telling someone whom you love that you love him (or her).

You get the idea, and you will certainly have your own examples. The caveat, of course, is that it is important not to take yourself too seriously. It doesn't matter if you can't learn to play Chopin within six months. It doesn't matter if you don't write poetry like David Whyte or Mary Oliver or speak like Mme. Zephir in high school French. It's about your intention and your commitment to take on a new experience that goes beyond where you are. Aliveness.

Reflection

- What's on your list? When have there been times when you have taken on some risk—big or small—on behalf of extending yourself beyond where you are? What have been your experiences... might there have been some sense of aliveness, even if your risks didn't turn out just as you expected?

- What's on your list going forward? What's holding you back from taking next steps with "Maybe sometime I'll..." "It would be really cool to..." "I've always wanted to..."?

Author

Linda Ellerbee (b. 1944) is an American journalist and writer. Beginning in radio, she transitioned to television news in the early 1970s, holding reporter and anchor jobs at both major broadcast and cable networks. She is particularly noted as the host of the long-running Nick News, a Peabody-award-winning news program for children that addressed important social and political issues and invited perspectives and commentaries from young people from around the world. Ellerbee has written three personal memoirs and several works of fiction. She is active in advocacy and support for women with breast cancer, arising from her own experience. The quotation comes from a book of interviews of notable women by Bonnie Miller Rubin, *Fifty on Fifty: Wisdom, Inspiration, and Reflections on Women's Lives Well Lived* (Warner Books, 1998).

PURPOSE

Frederic C. Craigie, Jr., Ph.D.

–10–

The heart of most spiritual practices is simply this:
Remember who you are. Remember what you love.
Remember what is sacred. Remember what is true.
Remember that you will die and that this day is a gift.
Remember how you wish to live.

Wayne Muller

In May of 1995, actor Christopher Reeve was taking part in an equestrian competition in Virginia when his horse abruptly stopped before a jump, throwing him forward onto the ground. Unable to break his fall because his hands were entangled with the reins, he landed on his head and suffered a broken neck. The former Superman, Reeve was paralyzed from the neck down for the remaining nine years of his life.

In the immediate aftermath of the injury, Reeve considered his profound disability and told his wife, Dana, that "maybe we should let me go." Her response was, "You're still you, and I love you."

Outwardly, of course, Reeve was not at all who he had been. Unable to walk or move, ventilator-dependent, relying on other people for personal care, the "you" of Christopher Reeve was very different. There was a core of who he had been that remained, however, that apparently blessed his family and fueled a busy life of activism on behalf of medical research and disability rights until his death.

"Remember who you are." The idea of who you are may not be called forth as starkly for any of us as it was for Reeve, but it is there. Both in the face of challenges and in the course of everyday life, there is a "you" that gives life direction and energy.

So... who *are* you? In my decades as a medical educator, I think the article that I have most often shared with trainees is "The Nature of Suffering and the Goals of Medicine," written by psychiatrist Eric Cassel and published in the *New England Journal of Medicine* in 1982. Cassel presents a short but elegant description of what it means to be a person: we all have a past, we have a cultural and social context, we have roles—and makes the case that we suffer when medical events disrupt the key elements of who we are. My roles, for instance, include being a husband, a father and grandfather, a psychologist, a neighbor and community member, a dog owner, a basketball player, a fiddler, a do-it-yourselfer around the house, and a 45-year Red Sox fan. A disruption of any of these roles would call for some accommodation and, to a lesser or greater extent, soul-searching. When I sprain my ankle playing basketball and I am out of action for six weeks, I suffer. When family members move across the country, I need to make some adjustments. (I can point out, by the way, that being a Red Sox fan prior to their 2004 World Series victory taught me a lot about suffering.)

But roles and social/cultural context do not adequately frame the essence of who you are. Muller wisely points out that the essence of who you are lies in your relationship with what is sacred for you. What you love.

Back up to the idea of roles. *Why* do any of your roles matter to you? *What is it* about being a sister, or a volunteer at the migrant shelter, or a nurse, or a tennis partner that matters to you? What are the underlying values that give energy and heart to the relationships in your life?

Reflecting on her roles as a mother, a community volunteer, and a part-time grant writer, a client said, "I guess they all have to do with putting a little goodness out into the world." This is good. Remembering that she is a person who brings goodness to the world is important for two reasons. First, it provides a values-based framework for looking at how she engages any of the activities in her life. "In my work as a Girl Scout leader, how am I doing with affirming and empowering these young girls?" Second, it provides a transcendent, enduring, and inalterable framework for being who she is even if circumstances change. Children leave home. Girl Scouts move on. Grant opportunities pass. But the opportunity to "bring goodness to the world" is always there.

Remember who you are.

Reflection

- Think of the key roles that you play in your life. How would you put into words why these roles matter to you? How would you put into words *how* you want to be, in serving these roles?

- What do you think that someone who knows and loves you would say about what they particularly admire about who you are and how you live your life? Do these qualities line up with what you see or what you value in yourself?

Frederic C. Craigie, Jr., Ph.D.

- In the week to come, pay attention to times when what you do—especially small, daily things—shows something of the best that you are.

Author

Wayne Muller (b. 1953) is, himself, a man of many roles: writer, speaker, and consultant, with particular interests in working with individuals and organizations to invite meaningful living and inspired leadership. A graduate of Harvard Divinity School, Muller has served as visiting scholar and faculty at the Fetzer Institute and the Institute for Noetic Sciences, and is the founder of two nonprofits dedicated to individual realization and community development. The quotation comes from *How, Then, Shall We Live? Four Simple Questions the Reveal the Beauty and Meaning of Our Lives* (Bantam, 1996).

-11-

You get this one life… If you do not have your deepest desires in sight-- and it's interesting that the word "desire" comes from the Old Latin, meaning "of the stars--" if you do not keep your star in sight, you're in danger of losing everything that is precious to you, and living out a life that is like a shell.

David Whyte

Remembering who you are is not an idle or academic exercise. You get this one life. Your desires are *of the stars.* Embracing who you are has a sense of urgency, of eternality.

What do you do that is *of the stars?* What choices do you make that align with the desires, the values, and the passions that are sacred for you?

Certainly, visioning is a part of the process. If your life is about compassion, you look for places where you can embody kindness and generosity. If your life is about curiosity and fascination with the way things work, you explore journalism or research. If your life is about understanding and honoring other people who are coming from different

Frederic C. Craigie, Jr., Ph.D.

places, you might sign up for the Peace Corps. If your life is about seeing the miracles and partaking of the joy of living, you might volunteer at a national park and spend your days in the natural world, or learn to play an instrument and spend your evenings in fellowship with other musicians. The possibilities are endless.

But the urgency and eternality of your deepest desires can be approached from the other direction, too.

Let me make a case for regret. Regret is one of those human experiences that can be terribly uncomfortable and remarkably useful. I regret not having done a foreign semester in college and missing out on fluency in a second language. I take pride in much of how I have been as a father, and I also have regrets of opportunities that I allowed to pass by. I think that I'm generally a pretty nice guy, but I regret times of impatience and unkindness. I'm part of a dying breed of professionals who have worked at one job for decades, and I sometimes wonder what it might have been like to have taken my skills and passions somewhere else.

Looking backward, regret needs a heathy combination of accountability and self-compassion. The adaptive role of regret—the energy of regret—lies in looking forward.

What have your shortcomings and failures taught you about what you need to learn? What do the times when you have been less than you fully are show you about your "deepest desires?" As you imagine approaching the end of the line, what will you hope that you will have done? What might you regret that you had not done?

I hold no illusions that we all can become anything we want. There are physical limitations—my days of dunking a basketball are over—and there are social, economic and cultural limitations. Doors are open for me as an educated white man that are closed for many other people. But within the circles where we travel, we do have choices about what we're going to do and about the qualities of spirit and heart with which we do it.

It's an urgent and eternal question; what do you do that is *of the stars?*

Reflection

- You may recall the last line from Mary Oliver's poem, *The Summer Day;* "Tell me, what is it you plan to do with your one wild and precious life?" (The poem in entirety is posted on the Library of Congress website, www.loc.gov.) What thoughts does this stimulate? What ideas form in your mind and heart?

- Notice, in the week to come, what you do that touches on your deepest desires about who you are. Big things—how you work on Tuesday on that project that you're passionate about—and everyday things—how you reach out on Thursday afternoon to the little boy next door.

- What do you think you might do going forward to further honor your deepest desires?

Author

David Whyte (b. 1955) is a Yorkshire-born poet, writer, and consultant. His poetry touches on the essential and often hidden and emerging qualities of soul. He is particularly noted for his consultation with individuals and teams in corporate settings such Boeing, AT&T and Toyota, where he invites people to form words to explore their own understanding of soul and expression of creative leadership. A dual British and American citizen, he lives in the Pacific Northwest. The quotation comes from an interview of Whyte on the PBS program, *Body & Soul with Gail Harris.*

-12-

We don't live for happiness; we live for holiness. Day to day, we seek out pleasure, but deep down, human beings are endowed with moral imagination. All human beings seek to lead lives, not just of pleasure, but of purpose, righteousness, and virtue. As John Stuart Mill put it, people have a responsibility to become more moral over time. The best life is oriented around the increasing excellence of the soul and is nourished by moral joy, the quiet sense of gratitude and tranquility that comes as a byproduct of successful moral struggle.

David Brooks

Michael Kent grew up among the few white people in a predominantly African-American neighborhood in Erie, Pennsylvania, where he was bullied by black children and his mother was assaulted by a black man. He became increasingly hateful of black people and eventually found a home in the neo-Nazi white supremacist movement. He attended rallies, recruited people to racist ideology, and was, himself, abusive and violent to non-whites. He found himself in and out of prison for theft, drug and weapons

63

charges. While in prison, he acquired a collection of racist tattoos—white pride and white supremacist symbols and swastikas (no, prisons don't offer tattoo parlors, but his buddies were creative with readily available substances and steel guitar strings).

When Michael was released from serving his last sentence, his probation was transferred to a black officer, Tiffany Whittier. Fearing his violent past, previous probation officers had visited Michael in pairs; Tiffany boldly came to his home by herself. This impressed Michael. She wasn't coming to judge him, she said, but he desperately needed a more positive direction for his life. Over time, Michael came to trust and respect Tiffany, and the two of them developed a relationship of accountability, support and, ultimately, friendship. At Tiffany's urging, Michael took down Nazi paraphernalia from his walls and replaced it with more positive images and, finally, underwent the painful process of having swastika tattoos removed. He landed a job where he was the only white man in a crew of over a dozen workers and came to value the friendship of his coworkers as well.

Michael comments, "If you have a strong support system, if you have people that believe in you in a positive way, you can change. She gave me the strength and courage to do what I'm doing... and changing my life because I know that if she can do it and believes in people, I know I can, too."

The journey of remembering who you are has a trajectory. It is always a journey of *becoming* who you are.

The unfolding of your life may not be as dramatic as it has been for Michael Kent, but you are on a journey, too, are you not?

Brooks uses the word, *moral*, not in the sense of a starched and sectarian caricature of a moral life (no dancing, please), but growing into an increasingly moral life in the sense of manifesting greater "purpose, righteousness, and virtue." He has also been writing for a number of years about what he calls "résumé virtues" and "eulogy virtues." Résumé virtues are the markers of a public life that signify achievement and success: becoming the regional vice president, being awarded tenure, joining the mega producers club at your real estate agency. Eulogy virtues are the markers of a life well-lived... the expressions of human goodness, courage, integrity and generosity that are extolled, for many of us, after we have moved on.

For me, there are some values and qualities about my life... the "moral," the "sacred"... that have remained fairly consistent over the years. With allowance for the imperfection of being human, I think I have always been absolutely devoted to my family, for instance. And there are other ways in which I have moved, and continue to move, into understanding and expressing who I am. I think I am more patient than I was years ago. I reach out more to people I don't know. My thoughts and energies are more occupied with the project of looking for ways to make a difference in the world.

How is this for you? What do you see of the trajectory of becoming who you are? How are you a different person than you were twenty years ago? Ten? Five?

"The best life is oriented around the increasing excellence of the soul..."

Reflection

- Think of a story that reflects a way in which you have grown in qualities of character, some way in which you are different—more attuned to the "moral" and "sacred" values of who you are—than you had been.

Frederic C. Craigie, Jr., Ph.D.

Sit with this story and recognize the courage and integrity that it shows.

• In the coming week, notice moments when what you say or do reflects your growth over time.

• A vital element of Michael's story is the role played by Tiffany Whittier. So often, the growth in our lives is prompted or inspired by someone else. Who has helped you to move toward "more excellence of soul?" Give thanks for that person. For whom do you pay the role of mentor and encourager?

Author

David Brooks (b. 1961) is an American journalist, writer, and commentator. He grew up in New York and Philadelphia, raised by parents whose lives showed him the passion of intellectual curiosity. At the University of Chicago, he struck up a relationship with the redoubtable William F. Buckley Jr., who invited him to work as an intern at the *National Review* following graduation. He spent several years at *The Wall Street Journal* as an editor and essayist before coming to *The New York Times* in 2003, where he writes a twice-weekly op-ed column on "politics, culture and the social sciences." Brooks has published several books of cultural commentary, including *The Road to Character* (Random House, 2015), which explores the development of the signature personal qualities of several prominent Americans—Frances Perkins, Dwight Eisenhower, Dorothy Day and others—from which the quotation comes.

– 13 –

Sometimes you have to play a long time to be able to play like yourself.

Miles Davis

I am a self-taught fiddle player. I think of myself as "intermediate." If you know traditional American music and heard me play *Whiskey Before Breakfast,* you'd probably at least recognize the tune, but you would not steer me in the direction of a recording contract.

After many years of trying to find my own way, I decided to take some lessons. Perhaps learning some of the foundational aspects of fiddle playing—how to position and hold the instrument, how to grasp and move the bow—would help me take it to the next level. I knew I didn't want violin lessons (yes, with some minor modifications: the "violin" and "fiddle" are the same instrument, but the approach to music is worlds apart), and I found a teacher who is a lover of old-time music and performer on fiddle and banjo. While he has indeed given me some tips on mechanical issues, his main message has been to relax and allow the music to come. Rather than approach music note-by-note and try to make it sound like some-body else's recording, first hear the music as I want it to be, as it resonates with me, and relax into allowing that music to come forth. I point out what a Zen approach this is, and he smiles. Thich Nhat Hanh meets Alison Krauss! You still would not steer me toward a recording contract, but at least the rendition of *Whiskey Before Breakfast* is now mine.

Making music brings me joy, but it is a sidelight in the larger picture of how I occupy myself. Musical notes on a foundation of spirit is an avocation; my vocation, on the same foundation of spirit, involves words.

Similar to musicians, speakers, and writers often talk about the evolution of their own Voice. I certainly see this in myself. My early speaking was stiff and formal and my early writing, in the places where psychologists write, faithfully adhered to writing standards but was not very inspiring. "Commenting on earlier meta-analytic reviews, Smith and Jones (1989) asserted that (blah blah blah)..." My early writing made for good bedtime reading for peo-ple who had a hard time falling asleep.

I don't believe I am now destined to win any literary awards, but I do take great pride in having developed a clearer and richer sense of who I am as a speaker and writ-er. I think of the way in which I use words as a conversation with somebody else. How would I speak with someone—with kindness, thoughtfulness, respect, compassion—one-on-one in my office? I try to hold this idea in mind and speak in the same way, and write in the same way. You will see, even in this reflection, elements of an informal style that I hope you experience as a conversation with you. First person. Contractions. Incomplete sentences. Ellipses. Sto-ries. Humor—not Jay Leno, gentle and often understated—but humor.

I gave a copy of my first book, several years ago, to a colleague whom I had not at that point met in person. When we finally got together, he commented that he came away from reading the book with a sense that he knew me. High praise.

What does it mean to you to "play like yourself?" How do you see yourself moving toward recognizing a unique voice that you can share with the world?

Might your voice come to life in artistic expression—your unique pottery, your unique cooking, your unique décor and landscaping? Might your unique voice come to life in how you move in your workplace and community as an advocate for the underserved or as an advocate for outside-the-box that no one else has thought about? Or might your unique voice come to life in how you relate to other people with kindness, with directness, with humor or with countless other qualities that together form a picture of who you are?

Recognize that the journey of being who you are... becoming who you are... is a journey of recognizing your unique voice, and coming to play like yourself.

Reflection

- How would someone who knows you put into words what makes you uniquely yourself? This question, by the way, would make for a good exercise: ask someone you trust, "I've been reading this book and let me ask you a question; there's this quotation from Miles Davis..."

- How do you think you are coming more to "play like yourself?" What does this mean to you, now?

- Notice times in the coming week when what you say or do represents your own unique voice.

Frederic C. Craigie, Jr., Ph.D.

Author

Miles Davis (1926-1991) was an American jazz trumpeter, composer, and band leader. He grew up in a relatively affluent African-American family in East St. Louis, the son of a music teacher and dentist. He was given his first trumpet by a patient of his father's, who also introduced him to the instrument and to the beginning elements of style of play. Davis made his way to Julliard but dropped out to perform full-time in the lively jazz scene in Harlem in the 1940s. During a 6-decade career, he was noted for his continuing, pioneering stylistic innovations, collaborating with and finding inspiration from many of the leading improvisational musicians of the times, from his early mentor Charlie Parker to more contemporary artists such as James Brown, Sly & The Family Stone, and Jimi Hendrix. Davis led a turbulent personal life, challenged by drug addiction, suffering failed relationships, and developing what his biographical site calls "a seething streetwise exterior that later earned him the title, Prince of Darkness." Much of his work is iconic in the world of jazz, notably the 1950 *Birth of the Cool* and the 1970 *Bitches Brew*. Davis won eight Grammy awards along with widespread public recognition, including an honorary Doctor of Music degree from the New England Conservatory of Music in 1986.

The quotation is reported both as "play like yourself" and "sound like yourself." I suspect that Davis phrased the idea both ways multiple times.

-14-

Throughout life, keep asking yourself, "What would I do right now, in this situation, if I were guided by my life purpose? What would I be doing differently at this moment?" The more mindful you are of your life purpose, the greater its impact will be on your life and the lives of those you care about.

Matthew McKay, John Forsyth, Georg Eifert

When I work with groups, I often begin with a mindful walking exercise. I give them Thich Nhat Hanh's instructions for walking meditation;

Take short steps in complete relaxation; go slowly with a smile on your lips, with your heart open to an experience of peace.

... and invite them to get up from their seats, leave the room, and return to their seats in a spirit of mindful walking.

The very first time I began a teaching session with a mindful walking exercise, years ago, I gently invited participants to get up and "walk around the room in a spirit of mindful walking." Not a good idea. It looked like *The Night of the Living Dead,* people walking stiffly in all different directions, bumping into each other. Mindful Walking 2.0 has been much better.

I present this exercise to emphasize the importance of *remembering* who you are, and to give people an experience of one practical approach to doing this. I want teaching session participants to return to the room being more fully grounded and present than they may otherwise have been, to be open to a greater awareness of who they are and why they are there.

Even as we may cultivate a rich sense of who we are in our quieter and more reflective moments, life has a way of leading...pulling...yanking...us off course. Perusing the online listing of a book on happiness and well-being recently (I try to keep up with these things), one of the customer comments was along the lines of, "There are some great ideas about calming practices, but this book assumes that I'm a free agent. I'd love to begin the day with a meditative time outdoors in the back yard, but I'm a mom and a professional; I need to get my kids who are not always cooperative ready for the day and I need to get myself ready for the day while my husband is charging around in the same spaces, getting himself ready for the day."

Does this, perhaps, sound familiar? None of us are really "free agents," right? Amid the daily expectations we might hold about how life would unfold, deals fall through. Traffic snarls. People are abrasive. Patients call at 4:55 on a Friday afternoon asking for a narcotics refill. And, of course, beyond the daily hassles that occur to a modestly comfortable, healthy white male professional, there is real suffering out there, as well.

The question is how you are going to remember who you are... to be faithful to the sacred and unique values and character that frame who you are... along the ups and downs of the journey.

I like the mindful walking practice because most of us do at least modest walking during the day and it is easy to make this, sometimes at least, an occasion for emotionally and spiritually pausing and centering. In the years of my busy practice and teaching, I didn't have time to meditate for 45 minutes during the day, but I did walk short distances, greeting people to speak with in my office, walking to the office of the teaching program, going down the hall to consult with a colleague, and heading (sometimes, I confess, with less than great enthusiasm) to a meeting, and I often used these opportunities to walk a little slower, to let go of the energy of whatever had just taken place, and to open my heart to what would take place next.

Many times, I have heard of similar practices from my physician colleagues. "Before I go into an exam room," one commented, "I pause for ten seconds, with my feet planted on the floor, and remind myself why I want to be there for the patient I am about to see."

Perhaps you have a similar practice, or perhaps you follow any of a number of other regular practices to "remember who you are:"

- morning devotions of reading and reflection;
- pausing before meals;
- journaling;
- meditation;
- prayer;
- periodic retreats; and/or

- engaging someone else—a friend, a book group, a support group—to provide accountability and caring along the journey.

May you find that your ongoing awareness of your purpose and unique character makes a difference for "your life and the lives of those you care about."

Reflection

- What have you done in the past to "remember who you are" that has been meaningful for you?

- Revisit a practice that has been part of your routine in the past, or explore a new practice in the coming week. It doesn't need to be fancy or elaborate. Pause to set an intention for the day. Choose an inspirational word or phrase and bring this to your attention periodically. Walk mindfully a couple of times a day. Sit quietly in a meditative spirit for five minutes. Go out in the back yard (or outside wherever you happen to live) and briefly open your senses and your heart to the experience of where you are.

Authors

Matthew McKay, Ph.D., John Forsyth, Ph.D., and Georg Eifert, Ph.D. are psychology professors who have long experience working with values- and mindfulness-based approaches to healing and wellness. Collectively, they have authored books on such subjects as happiness, self-esteem, and on therapeutic and self-help approaches to stress, anxiety, troubled relationships, anger and eating disorders. McKay is also the co-founder of New Harbinger Publications, a leading publisher since 1973 of both comprehensive resources for professionals and practical workbooks for the general public on self-help, health and wellness, relationships and personal growth. The quotation is from their 2010 book (New Harbinger, of course), *Your Life on Purpose: How to Find What Matters and Create the Life You Want.*

Frederic C. Craigie, Jr., Ph.D.

LAUGHTER AND JOY

Frederic C. Craigie, Jr., Ph.D.

-15-

When Native American medicine men talk to the sick, they usually ask three questions: When was the last time you sang? When was the last time you danced? When was the last time you told your story?

Frederic and Mary Ann Brussat

I grew up with loving parents who were passionate about music and whose tastes were... proper. My mother had been a professional opera singer in her younger years and played quite respectable classical piano into her seventies. My dad's piano proficiency was quite a bit south of his wife's, but he enjoyed playing and found his own niche and joy in performing choral music. When the radio was tuned to the Beatles and Monkees in my friend's homes, in my home, it was the Tchaikovsky Piano Concerto No. 1 in Bb minor.

When I was in seventh or eighth grade, my parents signed me up for after-school dance lessons, where Mr. Ciccorelli valiantly tried to teach his charges the Lindy and the Foxtrot. After going through the moves in slow motion, 1-2-3-4, for half an hour, we were "rewarded" by being al-

Frederic C. Craigie, Jr., Ph.D.

lowed to dance the Twist to 45 rpm records that classmates had brought in. Spare me! I despaired of wasting daylight hours doing anything other than playing baseball. My experience led me to put dancing in the same emotional category as going to the dentist to have cavities filled.

Over the years, this has changed. I recall going to a party in a barrio in Nogales, Sonora as part of a cultural exchange program—far from the world of Tchaikovsky—and joining in unscripted, improvisational, and joyful movement to the beat of Latin music. I danced at my children's weddings, following no rules or forms but making it up and partaking of the energy and spirit of being together with people I love. I have joined a smattering of Anglos dancing at a Tohono O'Odham singing/drumming circle in southern Arizona. Living for these many years in Maine, I've enjoyed contra dances. I have now come to see dancing as a joyful and freeing experience, as long as you don't take dancing or yourself too seriously.

So, when was the last time you danced? Or sang? Or picked up your ukulele? Or took pictures of flowers blossoming in the spring? Or paused to look at a cloudless night sky? Or shared some of the story about what you love... what you're passionate about... with someone else?

The journey of your life is serious business, in the sense of making thoughtful choices about how you use your time and fill your days. But "serious" does not mean "joyless." You are entitled to do things that bring you joy. You are allowed to do things that have no clear, immediate, redeeming purpose.

I do think that, as a culture, we conflate joy with what I'd call "distraction." Distraction means being involved with (largely passive) activities that fill the time and provide some respite from dealing with your real life. I'm sure that all of us enjoy some television and an occasional movie, but there's a point at which allowing these activities to dominate your life draws you away from being who you are and who you can be. And, of course, there is hollowness in the transient benefit of more seriously addictive behaviors.

Joy, on the other hand, has a quality of genuineness that distraction lacks. You can tell the difference, can't you? Joy is more, "This is who I am, this is what I'm passionate about, this is where I find pleasure, this is part of what it means to me to be really alive."

Reflection

- What brings you joy? What do you do that brings pleasure... energy... passion... into your life, even in the absence of any immediate socially-redeeming purpose?

- What do you recall in the past that has brought you joy, that may have slipped out of the picture in more recent times?

- How are you doing building such things into your schedule and routine? Is there an opportunity... and can you give yourself permission... to prioritize these activities a little more highly?

Authors

Frederic and Mary Ann Brussat have been writing and developing resources about spirituality and culture since the early 1970s. Frederic (whose name, I might add, is spelled the correct way) is ordained in the United Church of Christ, with a ministry focused on journalism and ministry. Mary Ann is an interfaith minister, ordained by the One Spirit Interfaith Seminary. Together, they have written extensively about spiritual perspectives and practices—their phrase is "spiritual literacy" –from world

spiritual and religious traditions. Their website, www.
spiritualityandpractice.com, provides over 40,000 pages
of content, bringing together much of their work: descriptions and resources for dozens of spiritual practices, hundreds of reviews of spiritually literate films, e-courses on
spiritual practices and formation, daily meditations, book
reviews (including several of their own), and a remarkable,
categorized, searchable, appropriately-cited database of
over 10,000 spiritually-pertinent quotations. They presently direct The Center for Spirituality & Practice in Claremont, California, affiliated with the interfaith-oriented
Claremont School of Theology.

-16-

An Apache myth tells of how the creator endowed human beings, the two-leggeds, with the ability to do everything—talk, run, see, and hear. But he was not satisfied until the two-leggeds could do just one thing more—laugh. And so men and women laughed and laughed and laughed. Then the creator said, "Now you are fit to live."

Larry Dossey

Laughter vitalizes the soul.

In the Navajo (or Diné) tradition, there is a sacred and joyful celebration of the First Laugh. When babies are born, they are understood to be part of two worlds: the Spirit world and the physical world. A baby's first laughter, often at around three months, is a sign of their transition to being fully present in the physical world as a member of their family and community.

The person who observes or elicits the first laugh... whose character is considered to be passed along to the child... is responsible for hosting an A'wee Chi'deedloh, the First Laugh ceremony. Guests offer food to the child, who responds (with the help of his or her benefactor) by sprinkling the food with salt crystals as a blessing for the guests and as a first expression of a life of generosity.

We are, certainly, hard-wired to laugh. I suspect that what we experience as humorous varies culturally, among families, and, of course, individually. Maybe you have never been able to relate to Uncle Bob's sense of humor, and maybe your family gatherings don't look like *My Big Fat Greek Wedding*, but you smile, and your eyes sparkle. As is the case with people across town and across the world.

Laughter, by the way, need not be in response to "things that are funny." There is growing international interest in Laughter Yoga, which is a practice that was developed by a physician from India in the mid-1990s. Laughter Yoga combines warmup activities and breathing exercises to invite group participants into the shared experience of laughter for its own benefit. No Marx brothers, no Jerry Seinfeld, just the shared and demonstrably joyful experience of a community of people laughing together.

The scientific literature (which is typically no laughing matter) about the empirical benefits of Laughter Yoga shows the common theme for non-mainstream approaches to wellness: "preliminary results are promising, but more research is needed." I suspect, though—as perhaps you do, too—that our grandmothers' wisdom of "a laugh a day" will turn out to be right on. If you're interested in exploring Laughter Yoga, you'll find clubs in most larger communities, and there are the customary postings of resources and video examples on the Internet.

From an infant's chortle to your own sense of humor to the pure experience of hearty laughter, laughter means you are fully human; it means you are fit to live.

Reflection

- How is laughter a part of your life? When was the last time you laughed heartily?

- Has laughter sometimes defused or redeemed difficult situations for you?

- How do you cultivate and express your sense of humor?

- In the week to come, notice your experience of laughter both privately and with other people. Are you happy with what you see, or might this part of your life warrant a little more attention?

Author

Larry Dossey, M.D., (b. 1940) is a physician, writer, and philosopher of science and the human experience. He received a traditional medical education, served with distinction as a battalion surgeon in Vietnam, and established and practiced in a large internal medicine group, serving as Chief of Staff in his affiliated hospital. As he recounts, he began to collect stories of "miracle cures" that opened up the possibility of far richer and more complicated human experience, neither understood nor studied, than his medical training had presumed. He began to study the roles of meaning, faith, prayer, and spirituality in health and healing. In the late 1980s, he introduced the idea of nonlocality, "nonlocal mind," which sees humans—and, indeed, all living systems—as connected in ways that are unbounded by time or space. The tantalizing early research on the benefits of distant intercessory prayer, for instance, reveals qualities of nonlocality as does the extraordinarily common experience of calling a loved one on the phone at the precise time they are calling you. Dossey's 2016 book,

Frederic C. Craigie, Jr., Ph.D.

One Mind, chronicles his continuing exploration of nonlocality, consciousness and the human spirit.

-17-

I don't want to get to the end of my life and find that I lived just the length of it. I want to have lived the width of it as well.

Diane Ackerman

Psychologists love to talk about depth. Depth psychology. Deeply-hidden instincts and motivations. Deeply-held values. Fine, but in a world with three (or more) dimensions, there is also length and width.

Between the two, I find that width is the far more intriguing. A widely-lived life invites and embraces passion. Enthusiasm. Sometimes, exuberance. You can be faithful to those deeply-held values, but you are also entitled to be passionate and to experience the thrill of being alive.

The 2007 film, *The Bucket List*, popularized the title phrase and made it part of everyday common language. Lead characters played by Jack Nicholson and Morgan Freeman, both terminally ill with lung cancer, craft a list of life experiences that that they want to be sure to have before they die—before they "kick the bucket." Some of the items on their list would be difficult for people without the bottomless financial resources of the Jack Nicholson character: sit on the Great Pyramids, spend a week at the Louvre, visit the Taj Mahal. Other items in the Justin Zackham script, though, are more accessible and testify beautifully to our fundamental shared humanity: witness something truly majestic, help a complete stranger, laugh until I cry.

Bucket list items draw you away from a narrow path. They involve new exploration, a broadening—widening— of who you are and how you find energy, renewal and joy.

Some of these items have always been a part of you. I knew in college that I wanted to have a life partner and children to love. Grandchildren, too, although getting to this piece of the bucket list required the complicity of my children.

Other items on your list emerge; you grow into them. My family never had pets when I was young, and I never gave much thought to the idea of sharing one's home with animals. As an adult, my wife and her sisters have taught me to love dogs, and now it is hard to imagine a home without the presence and unconditional love that our furry friends provide.

Your list, like that of the Jack Nicholson character, may include big ticket items; visiting Machu Picchu or Easter Island, cruising the rivers of Europe, or flying in a B-17. For me, a modest-ticket item that has brought me great joy has been hiking along Hadrian's Wall (followed, I might add, by the obligatory pint in the iconic Twice-Brewed Pub).

And your list may... should... include everyday experiences that have particular resonance for you; getting to know the three-year old next door, singing in front of other people, or learning enough Spanish to reach out, haltingly, to Hispanic people in your community who don't speak English.

The bucket list, by the way, operates in forward and reverse. The way we have come to use this phrase, we think of it as a listing of what we hope to experience in times to come. It can be equally meaningful, though—and often, affirming—to look at the bucket list items that have already been a part of your life.

The width of your life. Passion and exploration. Exuberance and creative intention. Extraordinary and everyday.

Reflection

- How do you think about the "width" of your life? What do you do that adds color and texture to the foundation of meaningful, value-based living?

- What excites you? Where have you found joy? When do you feel the thrill of being alive?

- List a few bucket list items that you have already experienced. Sit with the recollection of these experiences. How does it feel to recognize that in the midst of all of the other ups and downs these things have already been a part of your life?

- What is on your bucket list going forward? Along with items that would take some planning and resources, be sure to include items that you could seek out or experience tomorrow.

Author

Diane Ackerman (b. 1948) is a writer, poet, and naturalist. She knows what she's talking about as she describes a wide life. Along with a master's degree in Fine Arts, she received master's and doctorate degrees in English Literature, choosing for her dissertation supervisory committee a scientist (Carl Sagan, no less) together with a poet and an expert in comparative literature. The world, she felt, could not be understood from a single disciplinary perspective. She taught English and writing for a number of years and has contributed essays to *The New York Times*, *Smithsonian*, *National Geographic*, and the *New Yorker*, where she was a staff writer from 1988 to 1994. She has always been fascinated by the natural world (commenting in a 1999 interview that she lives with the wide eyes of an 11-year-old) and has traveled the world from the Amazon rain forest to Antarctica to study monkeys, whales, butterflies, seals, and seabirds. Ms. Ackerman is the author of over two dozen books of nonfiction and poetry, most famously in the public eye, her 2007 novel, *The Zookeepers' Wife*. She has received numerous awards, including being selected as a finalist for a Pulitzer Prize in 2012 for *One Hundred Names for Love*. She has also had a pilot's license for many years, with one of her books being a memoir of her experience of flight. I suspect the one thing she does not do is sleep. The quotation, by the way, comes from Linda Breen Pierce's book, *Simplicity Lessons* (Gallagher, 2003).

-18-

Like many academics, I spent my young adult years postponing many of the small things that I knew would make me happy, including reading novels for pleasure, learning to cook, taking a photography class, and joining a gym. I would do all of these things when I had time—when I finished school, when I had a job, when I was awarded tenure, and so on. I was fortunate enough to realize that I would never have time unless I made the time. And then the rest of my life began.

Christopher Peterson

When I met him, Tim was gingerly making his way back from a very serious heart attack. He had some specific ongoing deficits—I remember him talking particularly about diminished ability to write fluently—but mainly, he suffered from loss of stamina, chronic pain, and the constant shadow of his uncertain long-term future.

His story was remarkable for having had a near-death experience. He described many of the hallmarks that are typically reported in such experiences. He had been a detached observer of his care in the emergency room, seeing his lifeless body being treated, hearing staff speaking, and accurately describing specific features of the room, including many that he would have been unable to see from his physical position on a gurney. He described a tunnel leading to a bright, enveloping, welcoming light, and a feeling of infinite goodness and peace. And he described a recognition that it was not yet his time and that he needed to return to his life to love his wife.

Notably, Tim insisted that he had neither read nor heard about near death experiences. His story was his own.

He emerged from his heart attack and brush with death a changed man. Where, before, he had been upset by everyday annoyances-a plumbing problem, a computer glitch—he was now more "laid back," paying more attention to the larger priorities of his life: cuddling with his wife, pausing longer to talk with friends, and developing some new skills and passions to creatively accommodate to his limitations, like posting to eBay. His reflection: "You have to enjoy the ride, rather than get the ride done and then have a good time."

It's a common theme that I've heard many times. People change their priorities when they look mortality in the face.

It might be a cancer diagnosis that prompts such a heightened awareness of what really matters. It might be the death of a parent, where there are a few words you wish you had said. It might be pausing to imagine the suffering of a thousand people being killed in an earthquake halfway around the world. It might be finding yourself pacing when your newly-driving teenage daughter isn't home on time and doesn't pick up her cell phone.

Can you feel the tension in some of these scenes... or perhaps can you recall times when your life has provided you with a message of urgency about what really matters?

Weekly Soul

I suspect that all of us have had these moments. The compelling question, of course, is how we might invite that awareness and perspective into life without needing messages of urgency. After all, the experiences that you hope to have in your life have a time frame. They are limited-time offers. I won't hike down into the Grand Canyon when I'm 85. Your grandmother will only live so long. Your daughter will be a second-grader for only a year.

What would you do if you knew your time was limited or, more properly, what would you do if you carried with you the recognition that your time is limited? How might you try to engineer some big-ticket items that you have been putting off? How might you place greater priority on everyday expressions of self-care, passion, curiosity and laughter—along with the enduring qualities of kindness, generosity, and love?

Of course, you have serious commitments that you need to address. You have a job. You need to pay the mortgage. You need to cut the grass. But do recognize how easy it is to allow the exigencies of life to crowd out the things that bring you joy and restore your soul. You postpone the experiences that bring you life at your peril.

You are, again, entitled to enjoy your life. It is not selfish indulgence. It is not wasteful. It's your ride.

Reflection

- The tension is between doing what you need to do and creating time and space for self-care, passions, and joy. How do you see yourself managing his balance?

- Regret can be a useful experience as long as it prompts reflection and learning. When has there been a time when you have felt regret about having put off something that would have brought you joy?

Looking back, might you have handled this differently? Is there a point of learning here?

- In the week to come, do something that feeds your soul even if it means pausing with the daily requirements of your life. Walk the dog. Sit in a park. Jog. Read a book. Spend time with someone you love. Reflect on how this experience may help to bring more clarity to how you do such things going forward.

Author

Christopher Peterson, Ph.D. (1950-2012) was a distinguished academic psychologist, serving as the Arthur F. Thurnau professor of psychology at the University of Michigan. He was one of the founders of the Positive Psychology movement, joining with a small group of other psychologists in conducting seminal research about optimism, strengths of character and well-being. He died of sudden heart failure at the age of 62. An article of tribute in the journal *American Psychologist* describes him as "a distinguished scholar, an inspirational teacher, and a wonderful human being." He loved people, his colleagues say, with his qualities of humility, generosity, and attentiveness to others that earned him the nickname, "Mother Teresa." They conclude, "Although his scholarly contributions are significant, his lasting legacy will be what he shared with other people. So many of us are indebted to him for making us better researchers, better teachers, and better people." You can see an extensive collection of Dr. Peterson's blog posts, *The Good Life: Positive Psychology and What Makes Life Worth Living*—with a writing style that shows both scientific rigor and playful and joyful character—at www.psychologytoday.com/us/blog/the-good-life.   The quotation comes from his 2006 book, *A Primer in Positive Psychology* (Oxford Positive Psychology Series).

Frederic C. Craigie, Jr., Ph.D.

PRESENCE

Frederic C. Craigie, Jr., Ph.D.

-19-

When we let go of our battles and open our heart to things as they are, then we come to rest in the present moment. This is the beginning and the end of spiritual practice. Only in this moment can we discover that which is timeless. Only here can we find the love that we seek. Love in the past is simply memory, and love in the future is fantasy. Only in the reality of the present can we love, can we awaken, can we find peace and understanding and connection with ourselves and the world.

Jack Kornfield

Thanks substantially to work by Jack Kornfield, Jon Kabat-Zinn, Sharon Salzberg, and a small number of other pioneers in this area, the idea of mindfulness—paying attention, in the present moment, without judgment—has embedded itself in the American consciousness.

A man suffers flashbacks and remorse about a motor vehicle accident in which his drunk driving killed his best friend. A woman vacillates about flying out of state for a family wedding, worrying that she'd be so anxious that she'd "lose it" on the plane. A middle-aged electrician finds himself distracted at work by the significance of an elevated blood test, now out at the lab, from a routine physical yesterday. A Middle-Eastern refugee recounts his odyssey through settlement camps and is desperately concerned about the whereabouts of his two sons, from whom he had become separated. A young man takes a job as a flagger and berates himself for not having made choices that would have given him better opportunities. All of these people have work to do, but the common theme is that the redress for their acute distress is to be present.

When we experience emotional distress, our attention typically goes to a painful past or a fearsome future. We suffer with thoughts or images arising from what has been. We suffer with fears and uncertainties of what life might be.

The redress is mindfulness. Bringing our attention to the present moment. You can't change the past, and life is lived in a succession of present moments, not in what may or may not happen down the road.

The circumstances of life challenges and suffering are what they are and need attention. The driver needs to find a way to make peace with being responsible for his friend's death. The woman needs to develop a new perspective on the experience of anxiety. The electrician will need to see what the test result shows, and take it from there. The refugee spends hours pursuing contacts in searching for his sons. The flagger needs to train in a new skill.

Mindfulness will not itself alter the circumstances of these people's lives. What it does offer, though, is the possibility of a greater experience of peace and personal focus in the midst of those circumstances. When your attention is focused on this present moment, you reclaim control of your life from the feelings, memories and imaginings that would otherwise hold you in their grasp.

This moment, after all, is the reality of your life. It is what you have. It is all that you have.

This is your experience right now, whatever thoughts, feelings and images you may have. Can you allow these experiences to be there as you open your heart to this fleeting, irreplaceable, sacred moment?

Reflection

- Think of a time when you have been troubled and unsettled about your past or your future and when you found some found some respite in bringing your attention to the present moment. What was this like for you? Did this perhaps create in you a little different spirit of energy going forward?

- Experiment with this now. Call into attention some past suffering—a failing, a wound—or some future fear. Fill in the details of this past or future experience, and be aware of the feelings that it prompts. Now, direct your attention to this present moment. What do you notice?

- In the coming week, pause a few times—especially when you notice your attention drawn to a troubled past or uncertain future—to direct your attention and open your heart to this present moment.

Author

Jack Kornfield (b. 1945) has been instrumental in bringing Buddhist mindfulness practices to the West. After graduating from Dartmouth College, he served in the Peace Corps in the Mekong River valley in Thailand. He began studies with two Buddhist masters and trained as a

Frederic C. Craigie, Jr., Ph.D.

Buddhist monk in in Thailand, Burma, and India. Returning to the United States, Kornfield was a co-founder of the
Insight Meditation Society in Barre, Massachusetts and,
later, the Spirit Rock Meditation Center in Woodacre, California. He holds a Ph.D. in clinical psychology from the
Saybrook Institute. He lectures widely and is the author of
over a dozen books on Buddhist wisdom, mindfulness, and
meditation. The quotation comes from Kornfield's 1993
book, *A Path with Heart: A Guide Through the Perils and
Promises of Spiritual Life* (Bantam).

–20–

The quality of one's life depends on the quality of attention. Whatever you pay attention to will grow more important in your life.

Deepak Chopra

Achieving artistic and financial success by the early 1890s, Claude Monet purchased his home in Giverny, France and set to work developing a landscape that would inspire his painting in the last 30 years of his life. He received permission from local authorities to divert water from the Epte River to create a pond for cultivating water lilies. Monet spent long hours in his gardens, tending to them, and joyfully observing the constant unfolding of light, colors, and texture. He commented on his attention to his lily pond:

> It took me a while to understand my water lilies. I cultivated them without thinking about painting them. A landscape doesn't captivate you in just one day. And then, all of a sudden, I had a revelation: there was magic in my pond. I seized my

palette. Since that moment, I've scarcely painted any other subject.

Monet paid attention to his water lilies and they became—suddenly, magically—vitally important in his life.

Mindfulness means paying attention in this present moment. What we attend to grows. Where, then, do we direct attention?

Traditionally, the *meditative practices* part of mindfulness have involved directing attention to some point of focus. You may focus on your breath, a sacred word or phrase, or an image—leaves flowing on the soft current of a stream—and gently return your attention to this point of focus as your mind moves in other directions. There are centuries of healing narratives and hundreds of modern research explorations about the health and spiritual benefits of such practices.

Mindfulness as a *life practice* is involves both directing and inviting attention.

Inviting mindful attention means using all of your senses to be aware of the richness of your experience in this moment. For years, I've been teaching people what I call the "12 Things" exercise. You pause and quietly observe 12 things in your present experience: the feel of the chair where you're sitting; the temperature; if you're outside, perhaps a gentle breeze; the sound of voices in the hall or of a car passing by in the distance; the smell of springtime, the ocean, or your neighbor's barbecued ribs (vegetarians; imagine grilled leeks); and the awareness of thoughts ("Oh, isn't it interesting that I'm having the thought that I need to pick up milk on the way home!"). Twelve, of course, is arbitrary; the exercise invites a succession of experiences that come to you as you are curiously and observantly present and aware.

Directing mindful attention as a life practice means that you choose the parts of your experience to which you open your mind and your heart.

You can allow your attention to go to troubled emotions, past or future. You can allow your attention to go to the morning news of yet another school shooting, devastating flood, or precipitous drop in the Dow-Jones stock index. You can listen to the voices—I suspect we all have these voices—that tell you you're not good enough, or you can rehearse scenes of how you might exact retribution on someone who has wounded you.

Or, as a discipline to bring your heart back to a healing place, you can direct your attention to who you really are and what is sacred for you. "This is what surrounds me in my world right now. This is who I am and who I want to be."

What you attend to grows more important in your life. Monet's attention to his lily pond brought a revelation. Maybe mindful attention has some magic in store for you, as well.

Reflection

- Use all of your senses to notice your experience in this moment. What do you see, hear, and feel? Are you aware of particular scents or aromas? What do you notice outside of you, and what do you mindfully observe of thoughts, feelings, and images inside of you?

- Recognize that you have choices in where you will direct your attention in this present moment. As several clients have asked, what parts of your experience you want to "feed?" Where *do you* want to direct your attention and your heart?

Frederic C. Craigie, Jr., Ph.D.

• Pause a few times in the coming days to sit with the inviting (being aware of your experience) and directing (choosing where you want to focus your attention) aspects of mindfulness as a life practice.

Author

Deepak Chopra, M.D. (b. 1946) is an American physician, writer, speaker, and entrepreneur. He received a medical degree in India, where he was born, emigrated to the United States, and completed residency training in internal medicine and endocrinology. He practiced conventional Western medicine for a number of years before becoming disenchanted with its emphasis on pharmaceutical treatment and what he perceived as its limited scope of care. Chopra met Maharishi Mahesh Yogi, himself an early exponent of meditative practices in America, and partnered with him in developing the Maharishi Ayurveda Health Center and an affiliated business that marketed alternative health care products. He parted company with the Maharishi in the early 1990s, moved to California to direct the Sharp Institute for Human Potential and Mind/Body Medicine, and subsequently founded the Chopra Center for Well Being. His first of a long run of best-selling books, *Quantum Healing: Exploring the Frontiers of Mind/Body Medicine*, was published in 1989. In recent years, Chopra's writing and speaking have explored the role in healing of consciousness and quantum physics, and he has become prominent for his belief in the limitless potential of human wellness, healing, and aging. His work is certainly not without controversy, with some followers seeing him as a harbinger of a revolutionary approach to healing and some detractors seeing him as a New Age charlatan and criticizing his lucrative business of alternative medicine products and services. The quotation comes from Chopra's book,

Ageless Body, Timeless Mind: The Quantum Alternative to Growing Old, (Harmony, 1993).

Frederic C. Craigie, Jr., Ph.D.

In a time of drastic change one can be too preoccupied with what is ending or too obsessed with what seems to be beginning. In either case one loses touch with the present and with its obscure but dynamic possibilities. What really matters is openness, readiness, attention, courage to face risk. You do not need to know precisely what is happening or exactly where it is all going. What you need is to recognize the possibilities and challenges offered by the present moment, and to embrace them with courage, faith and hope.

Thomas Merton

A family physician tells the story of a frightening event in the practice's waiting room. A burly and disheveled man had become agitated and began to scream in an angry and threatening way. Other patients and staff scurried for cover. As the man continued his angry-eyed screaming, the one remaining patient, a short and frail elderly woman, walked up to the man, embraced him, and said "Oh, you poor, poor man." The man dissolved in tears, and the crisis was immediately defused.

Stories abound about people who make instant, heroic decisions without forethought to consequences. Your local newspaper, like mine, reports people who charge into burning buildings or dive into freezing rivers to save somebody. Uniformly, they later deny their heroism and say that "anybody would have done the same thing."

The present moment, as we have suggested, offers redress for past or future suffering and offers the opportunity to grow that part of our lives to which we direct our attention and heart. But there is more. The present moment is alive with possibilities. We choose not only where we're going to attend but also how we're going to live.

As Merton says, you don't know where your choice might lead. What matters is openness and courage, and they are sustained by faith. The key question of mindful action in this present moment is, "Who am I, right now, and what can I do that would honor the way I want to be living my life?"

I realize that's a mouthful, and that the exigencies of the situations in which we need to make these decisions usually don't allow thoughtful and calm self-reflection. But that is the question that anchors mindful action in the present moments of your life.

How are you going to respond to the angry person that you encounter? How are you going to respond to the destitute person you walk by on the street (or the person with the cardboard sign at the stoplight)? What are you going to do when a colleague tells an off-color joke? How forthright are you going to be about your strongly-held minority opinion with other people? How would it feel to express a clear "yes" or "no" to a request for your time about which you're ambivalent? Can you see yourself striking up a curious and open-hearted conversation with someone who holds very different social or political views?

There you are, as these moments present themselves to you. The grounding of your mindful action is mindful awareness and attention to who you are. You don't know how the consequences of your action will unfold, and, in fact, the more you wait for some sign of certainty, the more opportunities pass you by. The only assurances are that there is energy and aliveness in being faithful to who you are, and that there will be additional present moments of possibility to come.

Reflection

- When has there been a time when you did something meaningful on the spur of the moment without regard for the consequences? What was this like for you? What did you learn—or what was affirmed—in this experience?

- My examples above are of challenging and emotionally-charged situations, but there's another side of the coin. Think of a time when you have put yourself out there publicly—expressing humor, being creative, exploring something new, or otherwise being vulnerable—in a positive way. Same questions; what was this like, and what did you bring away from this experience?

- In the coming week, be aware of meaningful choice points. Notice, and then reflect on, how you respond.

Author

Thomas Merton (1915-1968) was an American monk, scholar, mystic and social activist. He was born in France to artist parents and made his way to Columbia University, where he was received into the Catholic church. After a short period of teaching English, he arrived in 1941 at

Frederic C. Craigie, Jr., Ph.D.

the Abbey of Gethsemani, a community of monks belonging to the Order of Cistercians of the Strict Observance (Trappists), which was to be his home for the remaining 27 years of his life. Along with being a gentle and incisive observer of the spiritual life, Merton was actively engaged in issues of social justice, particularly the 1960s peace movement and the nonviolent civil rights movement. In his later years, he also became committed to interfaith dialogue, meeting with world spiritual leaders such as the Dalai Lama and Thich Nhat Hanh, and publishing books on Zen Buddhism, Confucianism and Taoism. Among his several dozen other books are his bestselling 1948 autobiography *The Seven Storey Mountain*, and his 1949 spiritual classic, *Seeds of Contemplation.* The quotation comes *Conjectures of a Guilty Bystander* (Image, 1968).

– 22 –

Stay in the present moment. That's where you'll find life's magic... Sometimes to stay in the present we need to visit the past, to clear out an old feeling, to heal an old, limiting belief. But that visit can be brief. And sometimes we need to think about the future- to make commitments, to plan, to envision where we want to go. But to linger there can cause unrest. It can spoil the moment we're in now.

Melody Beattie

It is honorable and often spiritually enriching to be in the present moment, but this is balanced by compelling reasons to visit the past or envision the future.

Recently, I enjoyed a lovely evening bike ride along the Rillito River next to our seasonal home in Tucson. For people who haven't lived in the desert southwest, "river" means a dry wash that occasionally has flowing water if there is enough rain or snowmelt.

I found myself observing my own flow of thoughts. At times, I was very much in the moment, seeing the stunning beauty of the range of Catalina Mountains in the setting sun, experiencing the sensations of riding in my legs and arms and being aware of feeling blessed to be where I was, with the dear people who are in my life. At other times, I was aware of having ridden a couple hundred yards and having no recollection of doing so. I was mentally somewhere else, thinking about the next teaching session, the task list, and whether or not the Red Sox have enough pitching to make the playoffs again. Observing my thoughts in this way prompted the question of when it's appropriate to be in the moment—to be present to our current experience—and when it is not.

I am reminded of two thoughtful 2016 commentaries in the *New York Times Sunday Review*, making the case that there are good reasons sometimes not to be in the moment.

World-renowned psychologist Martin Seligman ("We Aren't Built to Live in the Moment," May 19) cites brain and social science research in making the case that for most people, thoughts frequently turn to future possibilities, and that this tendency is innate and beneficial. Seligman suggests that, more than "Homo Sapiens" ("wise man"), our species could be more aptly called "Homo Prospectus," in recognition of the central human role of considering future prospects. Your attention is well directed if you consider future options on a meaningful career path or, indeed, what else you'll need for tonight's taco salad dinner with Pat and Bob.

Journalist Ruth Whippman ("Actually, Let's Not Be in the Moment," November 26) presents a more philosophical argument. She suggests that that some present moments just aren't very compelling ("I'm making a failed attempt at 'mindful dishwashing'") and, more notably, argues that a focus on mindfulness can be an indulgence of material comfort and security that skirts around real sources of suffering:

> So, does the moment really deserve its many accolades? It is a philosophy likely to be more rewarding for those whose lives contain more privileged moments than grinding, humiliating or exhausting ones. Those for whom a given moment is more likely to be "sun-dappled yoga pose" than "hour 11 manning the deep-fat fryer."

So, when may it be helpful or meaningful to immerse ourselves in the present moment? (I'm back now; sorry, I was daydreaming for a few minutes.)

1. In suffering, as we have discussed.

2. In awe. Years ago, I remember the comment of a dear sister-in law that, in our culture, we too often rush to take photographs of things that inspire awe, rather than experiencing them.

> The world is filled with majesty, large and small; beholding the vastness of the Grand Canyon for the first time, seeing your child pulling herself up to a standing position, being greeted joyfully by your dog even after you've left him at home for eight hours. (It's beneath the dignity of most cats to show such reactions.), looking at the moon and knowing that people have been there, seeing the resilience of a man who has been though unspeakable horror in his home country to seek asylum in America, and is ready and willing to make a positive contribution to his new home. The list is endless.

In awe, being in the present moment means to pause to really experience such majesties and let them form as images in your soul.

3. With other people. How often have you been in a conversation with somebody else and found them focusing somewhere past your left shoulder? Not good. Being present to people honors them and, really, honors us all because it affirms the richness of humanity that is lived in relationships with other people. If you're in a conversation you don't like, learn some assertive skills to change the subject or make a graceful exit.

4. As a discipline. Finally, I suggest practicing being present: cultivating, by practice, the ability to be present. Pick a regular time... pick a random time... and just be where you are and be open to your experience. What do you see? What do you hear? What do you feel? What do you observe going on in your body? Your mind? You may become an explorer of majesties yet unknown.

So, may you invite your attention and your heart to the past, the future and to the present moments of your life in mindful ways that bring joy and honor to your unique journey.

Reflection

• Think of Beattie's comment that there are good reasons to visit the past or the future, but "to linger there can cause unrest." How would you put into words what makes your attention to the past or future meaningful and enlivening, rather than wasteful or demoralizing?

- And what is the flip side of this question; when do *you think* it is important to be in the present moment?

- In the coming week, experiment with intentionally visiting the past or the future as you would want to be doing. Notice what this is like. Then, gently bring your attention and your heart back to who you are, right now.

Author

Melody Beattie (b. 1948) is an American writer of books and other resources for self-help and personal growth. She is most widely recognized for popularizing the idea of "co-dependency," in which people fall into addictive, caretaking relationships with other people who are troubled and needy. Beattie knows whereof she speaks. She was sexually abused as a child, had developed serious problems with alcohol and other drugs by her middle and high school years, and had several arrests for drug-related offenses. A moment of spiritual awakening set her on a road to recovery, but she faced further struggles dealing with an alcoholic husband and with the tragic death of her 12-year old child in a skiing accident. She began writing, drawing out her passion for how people can come to understand and move beyond addictive relationships. Beattie has now published over a dozen books, most notably her 1986 bestseller, *Codependent No More*. The quotation comes from *Journey to the Heart* (HarperSanFrancisco, 1996).

Frederic C. Craigie, Jr., Ph.D.

When we make a place for silence, we make room for ourselves. By making room for silence, we resist the forces of the world which tell us to live an advertised life of surface appearances, instead of a discovered life—a life lived in contact with our senses, our feelings, our deepest thoughts and values.

Gunilla Norris

Silence is a rare and precious commodity.

It is rare because the world is filled with the sounds of modern industrial and commercial life. Unless you live in the Great North Woods of Maine or other similarly rural place, it is hard to escape the background din of motor vehicles. Your grocery store, your big box store, your local restaurant—all typically have background music that is so subtle and pervasive that you may hardly notice it. Like many people, you might have a radio on in your house for most of your waking hours. The world offers a constant stream of stimulation that may not involve physical sound but still intrudes in the same way. Count the people walking down the street with wires coming out of their ears or the parents at playgrounds staring at smartphones.

I have nothing against cars, background music, or smartphones, but I do wonder if we are uncomfortable with silence. I wonder if we are culturally so unaccustomed to silence that it is uncharted and potentially fearsome territory.

Silence is precious because "we make room for ourselves." In silence, there is an opportunity to hear an authentic voice—whether you experience this as your own wisdom and intuition or as the movement of a Presence that is beyond you.

Seeking silence is partly a matter of finding peaceful and quiet spaces: walking in nature or sitting in a church or synagogue. Nineteenth-century Americans regularly visited cemeteries as restful places for Sunday outings and picnics. When I was on sabbatical at Fuller Theological Seminary many years ago, I recall a prayer garden with a waterfall on one wall that attenuated the outside sounds of downtown Pasadena and made for a peaceful and reflective space.

Silence, broadly, is still available even in the absence of physical quiet. Silence is fundamentally a matter of quieting your mind and your soul so as to invite your present experience—being curious... being open... to your experience.

When I lead labyrinth walks, I suggest to participants that there are many ways of walking. Some people focus their attention on sacred words or phrases. Some people bring to the walk a particular issue or question in hopes of coming away with greater clarity or wisdom. My own practice is to come to the labyrinth without a particular focal point and without an agenda. I try to bring a curious, earnest openness to what I experience in the outer world and in my own inner-world thoughts, feelings, and images. Typically, something happens. Something comes, whether it may be put into words ("the placement of these small memorial stones along the path remind me that there is light in the darkness...") or whether it may be a feeling or impression (like gratefulness or blessedness) that is beyond words.

The labyrinths where I walk are generally peaceful and, of course, sacred places, but they are rarely silent. There is usually the sound of traffic and the awareness of people going about their business some distance away. The silence is of the heart. In this silence, we make room for ourselves.

Reflection

- Sit in silence for ten minutes. Just be aware of your experience. What is this like for you? When was the last time you did this (meditators, just go on now to Bullet 2)?

- Find a place near your home or workplace that offers a modestly peaceful and quiet environment. If you have not done so, visit there.

- Consider ways in which you could build a spiritual practice of quiet pausing into your life routine. You might pause incident to meals, to awakening or retiring, or to transitions in your daily activities. Try pausing and just being present before the weekly team meeting, yes?

- Choose a modestly *busy* environment, and experiment with quieting your mind and your soul. Can you "make room for yourself" and catch some glimpse of your "senses, feelings, and deepest thoughts and values?"

Frederic C. Craigie, Jr., Ph.D.

Author

Gunilla Norris (b. 1939) is a multi-national poet, writer, and psychotherapist. Her parents were in the Swedish diplomatic corps, and she grew up in Argentina, Sweden and the United States. Her writing includes eleven children's books, two books of poetry, and several books about spirituality, mindfulness and meditative practices. A continuing interest is what she calls "household spirituality, or the practice of spiritual awareness in the most mundane and simple of circumstances." The quotation comes from her 1992 book, *Sharing Silence: Meditation Practice and Mindful Living* (Bell Tower).

ACTIVISM

Frederic C. Craigie, Jr., Ph.D.

–24–

I want to pay tribute to people who have hope, who have always been kind of a minority, who are called "activists." "Activist" means what? Someone who does an act. In a democratic society, you're supposed to be an activist… you participate. It could be a letter written to an editor. It could be fighting for stoplights on a certain corner where kids cross. And it could be something for peace, or for civil rights, or for human rights. But once you become active in something, something happens to you. You get excited and suddenly you realize that you count.

Studs Terkel

In my counseling/consultation work, I often invite people to talk about what really matters to them. Consistently, I hear three responses. People often describe spiritual and religious relationships ("God;" "my faith;" "I'm not religious, but my spirituality is really important to me") and family relationships ("loving my wife;" "my children;" "being there for my aging parents"). The third—it warms my heart to hear this so regularly—is that people want to make a difference.

- I want to contribute to my community, give back to my community.

- It's important for me to care about people, to help somebody.

- I guess I just want to leave the world a little better for my having been a part of it.

As I tell groups as I talk about this, these are not beret-wearing left-wing existentialists from the East Village. They are regular people, embracing all of the diverse economic, ethnic, and cultural groups with whom I've been privileged to work.

For some people, the urge to make a difference takes form in activism as we are accustomed to think about it, working on behalf of large-scale social and political changes: a hunger strike for nuclear disarmament, a sit-in at a congressional office, or helping with voter registration in places with historically-disenfranchised minority communities.

The urge to make a difference takes form locally, as well. I see activism among my friends and colleagues:

- teaching meditation in a prison;

- starting a community group to develop fire preparedness plans;

- serving as a docent at a nature preserve;

- acting as a court-appointed special advocate for troubled young people;

- reaching out to invite new neighbors to dinner;

- attending meetings of the local planning board;

- preparing meals (and expressing welcome) at a shelter for asylum-seekers.

And yes, I think of a friend and colleague, now passed, who advocated for a lower speed limit in a village setting where children are often present.

As Terkel says, you are an activist if you act. The scale— the level, the focus—of your acting is less important than the simple fact that it is an expression of a commitment to human caring and connection.

In activism, broadly, you find two benefits. You influence the world, and "something happens to you." You come to a greater experience of aliveness yourself.

Reflection

- Think of a time when you have been an activist, when you have acted on behalf of larger or local issues. How do you see this having affected other people? What was the experience like for you, having done this?

- What opportunities for activism are out there for you now? Acknowledge for yourself the courage and devotion that underlie what you are doing now, and think about new possibilities for you to explore in the days and weeks ahead.

Author

Louis "Studs" Terkel (1912-2008) was an American writer, a radio and television presence, and a Chicago-based literary and cultural icon for most of the 20th century. He was born in New York and moved with his family to Chicago when he was a young child. In their new home, his parents ran a rooming house that gave Louis the opportunity to interact with a rich variety of people. He found more colorful characters in frequent visits to Bughouse Square, an open-air center for free speech and sidewalk oration. Listening to the breadth of stories in these places set Terkel on a lifetime path of curiosity about the human experience.

He graduated from law school—he never practiced law—and took the nickname "Studs" from the main character of the Depression-era "Studs Lonigan" trilogy by Chicago writer James T. Farrell. He began working in radio under the auspices of the Works Progress Administration's Federal Writers' Project and started a career of hosting radio and television programs in Chicago in 1944. During the McCarthy era, Terkel was backlisted for unapologetically speaking on behalf of progressive causes, supporting price and rent controls, opposing Jim Crow laws, and refusing to cooperate with the House Un-American Activities Committee. The hiatus in his professional life ended with the opportunity to move to station WFMT, where he hosted the daily music and interview show, *The Studs Terkel Program*, from 1952 until 1997.

Terkel's career as a writer blossomed in his late 50s, with the publication of a book based on interviews from his radio programs. This format of turning recorded conversations into print marked his finest writing over the years since that time: writing grounded in his unending curiosity about the life experiences of famous and ordinary people alike. His book of reminiscences about World War II, *The Good War*, won the Pulitzer Prize in 1985.

There is a searchable archive of over 1200 of Studs' radio interviews at https://studsterkel.wfmt.com/. This quotation comes from a 2003 interview in the PBS program, *Religion and Ethics Newsweekly*, about his book, *Hope Dies Last: Keeping the Faith in Troubled Times.*

-25-

Vocation does not mean a goal that I pursue. It means a calling that I hear. Before I can tell my life what I want to do with it, I must listen to my life telling me who I am. I must listen for the truths and values at the heart of my own identity, not the standards by which I must live... but the standards by which I cannot help but live if I am living my own life.

Parker Palmer

How do you spend your time? How do you choose how you spend your time? What undergirds your choices in how you spend your time?

Parker Palmer presents two scenarios. The first is when we embrace values and standards that are not ours. It's tempting, is it not, to be drawn along by the magnetic pull of cultural values? More responsibility is better than less. Higher remuneration is better than lower. Greater public prominence and recognition are better than doing things outside of the limelight.

Moreover, we can certainly pursue noble paths that are not our own. I know lawyers who don't like being lawyers and physicians who don't like being physicians.

The second scenario is when we hear a calling. Perhaps it arises from within ourselves, from a deep recognition of who we really are. Palmer calls this "the heart of my own identity." Perhaps it arises from the movement of a greater Presence or Spirit. Either way, an awareness of calling helps to frame and direct the ways in which we uniquely act in the world. This is vocation.

Vocation is a spiritual calling. Our modern word dates from the 13th century, from the Old French *vocacion,* a "call," a "consecration." The nature of this calling precedes the idea of vocation as a profession, but the idea of sacred calling and occupation or profession had merged together in word use by the mid-1500s.

Palmer himself, having earned a Ph.D. at Berkeley in the 1960s, wrestled for a number of years with his relationship with the academic world. He had advisors who told him that he would do well as a university professor and was destined to be a university president, but he was repelled by what he saw as the duplicity in values of higher education. He took a job mentoring students in community organizing but realized that he lacked enough of a personal experience of community for this to succeed. He left the academic world and spent ten years at Pendle Hill, a Quaker retreat center outside of Philadelphia. There, he came to two important realizations.

First, Palmer came to understand that his revulsion of the academic world was really less about the scarred values in academia and more about his own fears of failure to live up to the standards that the academic life would command. Being able to face the darkness in oneself, he says, is an important part of the journey.

Second, he recognized that the constant, life-giving thread of the work that really mattered to him was teaching. The calling—his vocation—was to teach, and this could be engaged best, for him, as an independent teacher and writer, apart from formal institutions.

When you listen to *your* life, what do you hear? What has your life been telling you about what you do well? What has your life been telling you about what you love to do? Vocation—a consecrated life—is formed in the coming-together of your emerging, growing answers to these two questions.

Reflection

- Life gives us messages in nudges and flashes. The nudges part... how, over time, have you experienced some gentle nudge or urging that invites you to move away from or toward some particular ways that you might spend your time? How have you come to an awareness that you really have inherent talents and passions for some things, more than others?

- The flashes part... when may there have been a time when you came to a more sudden recognition or unveiling of who you are and how you are called to act in the world?

- When you think of "calling" or "vocation," what does this mean to you right now? Think of a time in the last six weeks when this has been most clearly embodied in your life. How would you put this experience into words?

- In the coming week, notice two or three times when you are acting most clearly in concert with your understanding of vocation.

Frederic C. Craigie, Jr., Ph.D.

Author

Parker Palmer (b. 1939) is an American writer, educator and activist. His years at Pendle Hill and involvement with the Religious Society of Friends (Quakers) have been particularly formative for him, affirming his passion for teaching and for being a teacher of educators. Palmer speaks often about a seamless relationship between the inner life and the outer life—how we are both influencing the world from an understanding of who we are and are appropriating wisdom and insight from our life experiences. He is the founder and Senior Partner Emeritus of the Center for Courage and Renewal, which facilitates resources and retreats to create safe spaces of trust and exploration for individuals, teams and communities. The quotation is from Palmer's book, *Let Your Life Speak: Listening for the Voice of Vocation* (Jossey-Bass, 2000).

–26–

Not everyone is called to a life of service—at least, not in the most obvious sense of becoming a social worker or volunteering in a soup kitchen. Indeed, many who take that path soon realize that even these activities can become divorced from the rest of your life. Service, defined broadly, can be how you interact with each person and in each situation, no matter what the circumstances are.

Gerald Jampolsky

Before she became a best-selling author, Marianne Williamson had a job for a time as a cocktail waitress. She came to realize that the most important part of this work was not serving up drinks; it was reaching out and making a personal connection, one-by-one, with patrons. Reflecting on this understanding of service, she commented that every business could be "a front for a church."

You see this understanding of service reflected—or not—in what we call "service industries." My typical interaction with supermarket checkers, for instance, begins with them saying, "hihowareyoudidyoufindeverythingok,"

followed by an announcement of the total, and conclud-
ing with "hereyougohaveagoodday." When I smile and say
thank you, the customary closing is "no problem." Alas. In
fairness, the cohort of people who do this work tend to
be in their late teens, and I'm not sure that I would have
had the presence or confidence at that age to reach out to
middle-aged customers any better.

I imagine you have had the experience, though, of
workers in service industries who do make personal connections with you. There are some specialty or niche gro-
cers staffed by people a little farther along in years, who
tend to be more engaging. I remember a clerk at the rural
post office where we had a box for many years regularly
comparing notes about family, vacations, and the best reci-
pes for chicken salad.

Jampolsky's point particularly holds accountable those
of us who aspire to service in the sense of socially redemp-
tive roles. Whether you are a social worker or a community
volunteer, there is the opportunity to make a human connection with people that goes beyond the material facts
of your job. Indeed, in my long-time role as a psychologist, I think that the formal, documentable elements of my
work—setting goals, developing treatment plans, engaging
particular intervention approaches—may have been less
important than coming to people with a spirit of curiosity
and an open heart. Who are you? What do you care about?
What do you love? What brings you joy?

This is activism: recognizing that whatever your formal role might be, your activism is grounded in how you
interact with each person whose path you cross.

Weekly Soul

Reflection

- Call to mind a story of someone in a service industry who conveyed some interest in you as a person. How did this feel? What difference did this make for you?

- Recall, if you have had this experience, someone who provides service in what Jampolsky calls the "obvious sense" of community activism, whose work expresses genuine personal interest in people served. How do you think this human connection adds to the material aspects of their work?

- In the coming week, be mindful of how you interact with the people whose paths you cross, and recognize that this is activism.

Author

Gerald Jampolsky, M.D., (b. 1925) is an American psychiatrist and writer who is noted particularly for being the founder and leading voice of Attitudinal Healing. Suffering, in the Attitudinal Healing perspective, comes not from external circumstances but from judgmental and self-deprecatory attitudes. The premise is that there are only two fundamental human emotions; fear and love, and that the journey toward healing and health is one of letting go of fear and making decisions and life choices based on love. From its initial emphasis on children living with life-threatening illnesses and on HIV/AIDS, Attitudinal Healing has grown to provide free or financially-accessible services and education for children and adults at more than a hundred centers around the world. Often collaborating with his wife, Diane Cirincione, Ph.D., Jampolsky is the author of award-winning books including *Love is Letting Go of Fear* and *Forgiveness, The Greatest Healer of All.* The

Frederic C. Craigie, Jr., Ph.D.

quotation comes from a 2002 interview of Jampolsky by
Drs. Cassandra Vieten and Tina Amorok, reported in their
book, *Living Deeply: The Art & Science of Transformation
in Everyday Life* (New Harbinger, 2007).

–27–

*Love is another word that is a bit (or a lot) ruined-
something we routinely speak of as something we fall
into and fall out of. But as a piece of intelligence about
what makes us human, and what we are capable of,
it is a virtue and way of being we have scarcely begun
to mine. People who have turned the world on its axis
across history have called humanity to love. It's time to
dare this more bravely in our midst, and dare learning
together how love can be practical, creative, and
sustained as a social good.*

Krista Tippett

Love can change the world.

There is the rippling, accumulative effect of treating each person you meet with dignity and grace, but there is more. Creatively applied, love fuels activism that reconfigures the world in the public sphere, as it does among individuals.

Jonathan Cedar is a professional engineer and avid camper. Weary of the difficulty of rationing gas and batteries on long camping excursions, he and friends set out to develop small, energy-efficient woodstoves that would run on the sticks and branches that were usually abundant on the trail.

As their idea and product developed, they realized broad applications in the less-developed parts of the world. They learned that half of the people on earth cook over open fires, with staggering personal and ecological costs. The WHO estimates that 4 million people die annually from wood smoke exposure, largely women and children, who are principally exposed to cooking fires. Wood fires, moreover, account for 25% of global black carbon emissions, more than all the world's motor vehicles. They also learned that increasing numbers of these people have access to cellphones but often have to travel for hours to access electricity to recharge them.

It occurred to them that they potentially had two distinct markets that were tied together by the common need for off-the-grid energy; first-world outdoor enthusiasts and rural people in developing countries. Cedar and colleagues create a business model that they call "parallel innovation," whereby profits from sale to the relatively-affluent hikers and campers are used to underwrite product distribution and discounted sales in India and sub-Saharan Africa. Their company, BioLite, produces a variety of products, but the flagship product is their original camp stove that provides smokeless cooking fire and a USB-port electrical connection for powering a small light and charging gear. This is convenient for the outdoor enthusiasts and life-giving for people who have never had access to such resources. Through social entrepreneurship and reaching out in caring and compassion to affirm the dignity and empower the lives of other people in a sustainable and mutually-beneficial way, love changes the world for two groups of people half a world away, as I imagine it surely does for the developers who make this happen.

I see the transformative effects of love all around: the Afghan-refugee Lyft driver who makes a point to invite new neighbors to dinner, creating a spirit of community among people from all walks of life; the physician and social worker in rural Maine who have created a culture in their primary care practice where employees feel safe and affirmed to bring their whole selves to work and where patients can feel a spirit of welcome and hospitality; and the nonprofit CEO who works tirelessly on behalf of statewide and regional health care access. At the largest social levels, my experience in the antiwar movement in the 1960s was that it certainly witnessed the complete range of human emotion, ultimately fueled by love, in the widespread dream that we really could create a better, more compassionate world.

One of my heroes is Ernest Saunders. I knew Ernest, now long passed, in his retirement after a distinguished career as a theologian and seminary professor. I remember asking him, as we washed dishes together after a public supper, how he would put into words the meaning of *agape*, the highest and most humanly generative form of love among the several words that the ancient Greeks used to describe love. His response: "living toward other people so that they can become all that they have been created to be."

Love touches the hearts of individuals, and love—personally and structurally—changes the world.

Reflection

- How have you seen love as a "social good," creating opportunities for people or forming more compassionate cultural relationships?

- What qualities do you see in people whose grounding in love begins to transform some part of the world? How do you see these qualities in yourself?

- What do you think about Dr. Saunders' comment about agape? How do you... how might you... "live toward other people" so that they can become all that they have been created to be?"

Author

Krista Tippett (b. 1960) is an American journalist, writer, radio host, and, herself, a social entrepreneur. After college, she was awarded a Fulbright scholarship to study in Germany. Subsequently, she worked as an independent journalist and then served as an aide in the State Department in Berlin.

Tippett earned a Masters of Divinity degree from Yale and hatched the idea of a radio conversation about spirituality and religion in everyday life. *Speaking of Faith* began on Minnesota Public Radio and evolved into her signature program, *On Being*. Its website describes the program: it "takes up the great questions of meaning in 21st-century lives and at the intersection of spiritual inquiry, science, social healing, and the arts. What does it mean to be human, how do we want to live, and who will we be to each other?" Podcasts of *On Being* have now been downloaded over 200 million times.

In 2013, Tippett began a non-profit production enterprise, Krista Tippett Public Productions (KTPP), and debuted the Civil Conversations Project, which orchestrates dialogue about challenging issues with the foundation of six "grounding virtues; "adventurous civility," "hospitality," "generous listening," "patience," "humility," and "words that matter."

Her books are *Einstein's God: Conversations about Science and the Human Spirit, Speaking of Faith: Why Religion Matters and How to Talk about it,* and *Becoming Wise: An Inquiry into the Mystery and Art of Living* (Penguin, 2016), from which the quotation comes.

Frederic C. Craigie, Jr., Ph.D.

ACCEPTANCE

Frederic C. Craigie, Jr., Ph.D.

-28-

Why bother accepting reality? Why confront helplessness, terror or losses? Why not distract ourselves as much as possible from the inevitable destruction that awaits us and all we love? Spiritual and religious teachers say that a full embrace of reality, in all its glory and horror is the only way out of even greater suffering. This is not an idea that enjoy popularity in our secular culture. Popular culture encourages people to distract themselves from ultimate reality with work, achievement, financial success, internet surfing and sports... people are frantically rowing toward something or someone who will get them out of their pain. Spiritual traditions teach people to let go of this pointless venture. Only the individual who can embrace reality as it is will find peace of mind, equanimity or a state of grace.

Cynthia Sanderson

I collect folk wisdom and stories of resilience. A phrase I often hear from people facing serious and often inalterable life challenges is, "It is what it is."

Frederic C. Craigie, Jr., Ph.D.

For a number of years after the Iraq war, our community in Maine saw a modest influx of refugees who had fled their country because their politics or their religion had made them unwelcome in their homes. Many of them skilled or professional workers, they told stories of arduous journeys involving long treks on foot, family separations, and crowded tent refugee camps on their ways to America.

One man whom I felt privileged to meet had been an engineer in Iraq. With the support of local general assistance, he was struggling to get back on his feet, living in a marginal apartment among other expatriates from his country. His two daughters had become separated from him and his wife in passing through a camp in Turkey, and he had no idea where they might now be. He had other extended family members who had remained in Iraq, and he was gravely concerned for their safety. Nor were his troubles limited to issues of immigration; both his wife and a daughter who had traveled with them had significant health issues that required substantial medical care.

Reflecting on all of his hardships, his comment was "that's just how it is." "Everyone has problems," he continued, "but you can live moaning and worrying, or you can live. When I hear of problems in Iraq and worry about my family there, I hold my head and remind myself to keep my brain in a good situation, not for myself but to make good decisions for my family... Even though there are dark things, even in the midst of darkness, you have to live."

This is acceptance.

Acceptance does not mean approval, endorsement, or gladness. My friend's preferred script for his life would never include displacement from his home, separation from his daughters whom he loves, or grave illnesses in his family in America.

Acceptance does not mean an absence of distressed emotions or shallow and silly positivity. We are all gifted with the ability to feel, and grief... anguish... anger... are part of the human condition.

Acceptance does not mean passivity. My friend writes letters and calls consulates seeking the whereabouts of his daughters. He is an advocate for his wife and third daughter in the health care system. He studies and finds comfort in the Qur'an. And all the while, he is engaged in relationships with his friends and community.

Acceptance means recognizing reality for what it is. Looking at it in the face, rather than looking away. Having emotions but not letting them call the shots.

The fruitless quest to resist, deny, or avoid reality takes energy away from living your life. The alternative, as my Iraqi friend teaches me, is to embrace your reality as it is and to keep sight of who you are and how you are called to live.

Reflection

- Think of a point of suffering for you. What does it mean to "accept" (Sanderson also introduces the word, "embrace") this reality?

- There is no spiritual depravity in watching some television or videos on your smartphone. Where, however, do you draw the line between innocuous down time and distraction that draws you away from who you really are?

- Notice your reactions to the ongoing or new challenges that you face in the coming week. Consider the idea that accepting these challenges—seeing them as they are—frees you to creatively address them.

Frederic C. Craigie, Jr., Ph.D.

Author

Cynthia Sanderson, Ph.D. (d. 2003) was an American psychologist and educator. She served much of her career at New York Presbyterian Hospital and, at the time of her passing, was Director of Training at Behavioral Tech, LLC. Cindy, as her friends and colleagues knew her, was actively involved in a network of psychologists who pursued clinical practice and research about dialectical behavior therapy ("DBT"), one of a number of recent approaches to behavior therapy, focusing particularly on helping people to develop the ability to tolerate distress. She apparently knew whereof she spoke. Her death came after a many-year struggle with breast cancer, and her own journey of acceptance is cited in her *New York Times* obituary:

> She lived a vital life filled with great love for her daughter, family and friends. Some months before Cindy's death, she wrote to a friend, "I stood out on the back porch this afternoon and I prayed for the peace and grace to accept this life on its own terms...to have the courage and the will to do just that."

The quotation comes from Sanderson's collaboration with two visionary psychologists. It is excerpted from the chapter, "Acceptance and Forgiveness," written with Marsha Linehan, Ph.D., in *Integrating Spirituality into Treatment*, edited by William R. Miller, Ph.D. (APA, 1999). Linehan is the developer of DBT. Miller is the principal developer of the widely-used protocol for lifestyle change, Motivational Interviewing.

–29–

Life is a choice. Psychological pain is not a choice.
Either way you go, you will have problems and pain. So,
the choice here is not about whether to have pain. The
choice is whether or not to live a meaningful life.

Steven C. Hayes

We all suffer.

The life free of distress and suffering is illusory, or, at least, the quest to avoid psychological pain leaves you spiritually hollow. Want to avoid anxiety? Don't try anything new. Want to avoid sadness? Don't do anything where you could fail. Want to avoid grief? Don't have relationships.

You may see people out there who seem to have lives of unbridled happiness and joy, but as you look closely, you'll find that their experience is more about transformation of suffering than the absence of suffering. No less a joyful spirit than His Holiness the Dalai Lama speaks of times when his own path has been enriched as he has experienced sadness and grief.

As well, there are the sad stories of people who look jaunty and ebullient to all the world but who wrestle with

Frederic C. Craigie, Jr., Ph.D.

their own demons inside. You may recall the death of Robin Williams, whose public persona was one of constant gaiety and mirth but whose interior life was apparently so intolerable that he committed suicide.

Whether to experience psychological pain is not an option. It is. It will be. The choice is in how we respond to that suffering.

My friend and long-time associate Ken Hamilton, M.D., is a former surgeon who has dedicated the last several decades of his life to developing a network of support groups that offer communities of hope and healing in the face of all manner of adversity. He may be described as "the Bernie Siegel of Maine" although I prefer to locate Bernie Siegel as "the Ken Hamilton of Connecticut."

Ken says, "This is what your life is giving you. Now, what are you going to do with your life?"

The psychological distress we all face—unsettling thoughts, hard feelings, disturbing images—just appear on the doorstep for reasons that sometimes are clear and sometimes not. The challenge is to develop the ability to have these experiences, to tolerate the distress of these experiences, and still to make choices in the direction of living a meaningful life.

Life is giving you a detached and often unfairly critical boss, and you're angry. It is what it is. You accept this, you face this. Now, what are you going to do with your life? What are you going to do that aligns with your deepest values?

Life is giving you a financial downturn or a serious illness, and you're fearful. It is what it is. You accept this; you face this. Now, what are you going to do with your life? What are you going to do that aligns with your deepest values?

Heaven forbid, life takes away from you someone you dearly love, and you grieve. It is what it is. You accept this; you face this. Now, what are you going to do with your life? What are you going to do that aligns with your deepest values?

Acceptance is not about smooth sailing or easy choices. You can tremble with fear. You can rage against the Universe. But part of the blessing of your humanity is that even as you sit with the suffering that you feel, you have the ability to choose how you carry on.

Reflection

- The sad story of Robin Williams—a tragedy that the world has lost this person—calls to mind the peril of comparing ourselves unfavorably to people who seem to have it all together. At the same time, most of us have people in our lives who mentor or model dignity and resilience in the face of suffering. Who has there been for you who teaches you about facing and responding meaningfully to suffering?

- When has there been a time in your experience when you have been able to face—accept—psychological pain and gather the energy of your heart and soul to respond to this suffering in ways that show the best of who you are?

- In the coming week, notice how you respond to unpleasant and painful thoughts, feelings, or images. What do your responses show or teach you about acceptance and making meaningful choices?

Author

Steven C. Hayes, Ph.D. (b. 1948) is an American psychologist and educator, based in the Department of Psychology at the University of Nevada. A prolific researcher and writer, he has authored dozens of books and several hundred journal articles. He is the developer of Relational Frame Theory, which has been the theoretical basis for the development of Acceptance and Commitment Therapy, an empirically-based counseling approach that merges mindfulness with values-based action. Hayes has held most of the pertinent leadership positions in the world of applied behavior therapy and has garnered a collection of lifetime achievement awards in his field. The quotation comes from his seminal popular-press workbook, *Get out of Your Mind and into Your Life: The New Acceptance and Commitment Therapy* (New Harbinger, 2005).

-30-

*Man can preserve a vestige of spiritual freedom, of
independence of mind, even in terrible conditions
of psychic and physical stress. We who lived in
concentration camps can remember the men who
walked through the huts comforting others, giving away
their last piece of bread... they offer sufficient proof that
everything can be taken from a man but one thing: the
last of the human freedoms—to choose one's attitude
in any given set of circumstances, to choose one's own
way. It is this spiritual freedom – which cannot be taken
away—that makes life meaningful and purposeful.*

Viktor Frankl

As I speak with people who are going through all sorts
of life challenges, I sometimes ask, "If you knew it would
be OK... if you knew it would turn out OK... would that be
OK? (Acknowledgment to Martin Van Buren, by the way,
who, as legend has it, coined the term.)

People find this an easy question to answer, and the
response is always "yes." The follow up question is not so
easy; "What has to happen in order for it to be OK?"

This moves the conversation to the realm of attitudes and beliefs. Acceptance begins with attitudes and beliefs. Meaningful life choices start with attitudes and beliefs.

The initial part of the conversation, of course, often has to do with control. You can't require an outcome that you can't control. "She has to apologize." "My fibromyalgia has to go away." "I have to get the job." Heart-felt as such hopes may be, they stand in the way of acceptance and creative resilience.

Beyond the issue of control, people often come to recognize that their emotions and responses in difficult situations are driven by attitudes and beliefs about themselves. When we are emotionally challenged, we often experience, largely unbidden, all manner of self-deprecatory, disempowering, and pessimistic thoughts and attitudes:

- I'm not good enough.

- Nothing I do matters.

- I deserve to suffer.

- Why bother?

These are crippling attitudes. And they are not true. Life-giving attitudes are different.

- It is a quality of your humanness to sometimes fail or fall short.

- You are formed but never compelled by your history.

- You can make choices.

- Small acts of goodness matter.

You can choose your attitude—some psychological literature uses the term "self-instruction"—and your attitude is the basis of how you choose to act.

Frankl, an Austrian Jew and a psychiatrist who survived concentration camps during the Holocaust, was inspired by fellow prisoners who chose not to be powerless in the face of unspeakable dehumanization. Giving away morsels of bread is a radical act, grounded in the attitude that the ability to make choices can't be taken away.

Acceptance and creative resilience begin with attitudes, with recognizing and affirming the truth about your life.

Reflection

- Recall a time when you felt demoralized. What was your belief at the time about what would need to happen in order for it to turn out OK? How would you answer the question in a similar situation now?

- I've given you four examples of "life-giving" attitudes above. What would be on your list?

- In the coming week, listen for the unbidden thoughts that come to you in challenging times. Pause to remind yourself that you can choose how you are going to respond. Orient yourself to your own life-giving attitudes as the basis for what you do.

Author

Viktor Frankl, M.D., Ph.D. (1905-1997) began to develop his signature psychotherapeutic approach prior to the Second World War and came to a richer understanding growing out of his own concentration camp experiences. "Logotherapy" (the term comes from the Greek *logos;* "reason") is based on the premise that the primary human motivating and empowering force is the journey of finding meaning in life experience.

Frederic C. Craigie, Jr., Ph.D.

From his earliest adult years, Frankl was interested in the issues of philosophy, meaning, and values. He gave his first public lecture, "On the Meaning of Life," at the tender age of 16. He completed medical training and engaged in lively correspondence about the interface of psychology and philosophy with Sigmund Freud and Alfred Adler. The focus of Frankl's clinical work before the war was with young people, opening free clinics for adolescents in several European cities, and directing a program of suicide prevention.

As the Nazi presence in Austria took hold in the late 1930s, Frankl was forbidden to practice with non-Jews. He became director of a clinic for Jewish patients, where he falsified diagnoses to save patients from selection for execution. The protection afforded by his professional status could only buy him so much time; in 1942, Frankl and his family were arrested and sent to Theresienstadt Ghetto and then on to concentration camps. His wife, mother, and brother died at Auschwitz. Frankl himself was moved among different concentration camps, then liberated at Dachau in the spring of 1945. He was, as the quotation suggests, a keen observer of defeat and resilience in camp life. He maintained his own sanity in his internment—and found some degree of personal meaning—by reconstructing a lost pre-war book manuscript on stolen fragments of paper.

In a furious burst of effort reminiscent of Handel's one-month completion of *The Messiah*, Frankl wrote his world-renowned classic, *Man's Search for Meaning*, in nine days in 1946. The first edition in the United States was published in 1959.

The remainder of Frankl's life was devoted to the further development and elaboration of his ideas about meaning and well-being, in his writing and in guest professorships in Europe and America.

The quotation is from *Man's Search for Meaning*.

Frederic C. Craigie, Jr., Ph.D.

-31-

It may be that when we no longer know what to do, we have come to our real work and when we no longer know which way to go, we have begun our real journey. The mind that is not baffled is not employed. The impeded stream is the one that sings.

Wendell Berry

Bill Wilson looked at his life and recognized that it wasn't working. He was deeply depressed and in the grip of severe addiction to alcohol. He recounts that he "gagged badly" on the idea of a Power Greater than himself, but cried out that if there were a God, that God would come to him and that he would do anything God might ask in order to change his life. Suddenly, he experienced a "great white light;" he felt a spirit of ecstasy and transformation and realized that he was a free man. Known widely as "Bill W.," he became one of the two co-founders of Alcoholics Anonymous, which now offers over 100,000 groups with over two million active members worldwide.

Acceptance is more than developing the ability to tolerate distress. Acceptance can prompt transformation.

Frederic C. Craigie, Jr., Ph.D.

For some people, transformation arises out of despair: substance abuse, failed relationships, and life-compromising illness.

For other people, transformation arises—suddenly or gradually—with the recognition that life isn't terrible but also doesn't bring much satisfaction or joy. I have lost count of the people I've worked with who have left jobs in which they were materially comfortable but spiritually dead, like the young man who left a modestly lucrative position with a beverage distributor when he realized that he didn't want to spend his life "selling people sugar water that they don't need."

Rarely, I find, do people who are on a journey of transformation away from suffering have a clearly-mapped future. You may have a clear image of Plan A in the rear-view mirror but not of Plan B on the road ahead.

It is at this point of recognizing that you don't know what to do or where to do it that "the real work" begins. What is "the real work?"

- Being willing to leave the familiarity of the old life behind. Familiarity brings comfort and security, even in the setting of suffering.

- Soul searching; earnestly exploring the question of who you are and what you genuinely want in your life. What do you care about? What brings you joy? When have you felt really alive? What do you know, and what do you do well? Questions like these.

- Being willing to embrace the uncertainty and ambiguity of a new way of being. Being curious and attentive about doors that close and doors that open. Bill Wilson had no idea on December 11, 1934 (the date of what is known as his "white light" experience) what a life of sobriety might bring. The beverage distributor had no idea where his new life would take him and certainly would not have imagined that he would find himself happily directing a program of Big Brothers/Big Sisters. At the point of not knowing where to go, demanding to have a clear and certain new path only stifles the creative new journey.

Not knowing what to do or where to go is not a failure. It need not be the dead end that it may well seem to be. It's an open palette, and the colors are all out there, waiting for the real work to form them together.

Reflection

- Recall a time when you were at a point of not knowing what to do or where to go. Perhaps in a job. Perhaps in a relationship. Perhaps, like Bill W, in relation to how you had been living your own life. As you think about what "acceptance" may have meant in that circumstance, what was "the real work"—the soul-searching about what really mattered to you and sitting with the uncertainty about what the future might hold? How did you navigate the journey of closed and open doors going forward?

- Consider whether there is someone you know who has faced what seemed like a dead-end circumstance and handled it with grace, perhaps, even, finding some healing or spiritual growth along the way. What can you learn from that person's journey?

- In the week to come, pause in some circumstance when you feel "at a loss" about how to proceed. Think about what really matters to you and how you might move forward in ways that align with your values about who you are. Practice letting go of expectations of certainty as you chart the path that you need to follow.

Author

Wendell Berry (b. 1934) is an American writer, poet, and essayist. He is a man of many talents and passions. He is internationally prominent in the world of letters, his books of poetry, fiction, and essays having garnered wide recognition and numerous awards. He is a devoted small-scale organic farmer, returning to his birth state of Kentucky in the mid-sixties to buy a farm in the region where his parents' families had themselves farmed for over five generations. And he is an activist and advocate for many causes, demonstrating on behalf of concerns about the Vietnam War, nuclear power, the death penalty, coal-fired power generation, and national security strategy in the wake of the World Trade Center attacks. Continuing themes in his writing have been the importance of sustainable human connections with the earth and the importance of community.

The quotation, among the most prominent snippets of Berry's voluminous work, comes from his essay, "Poetry and Marriage," in *Standing by Words* (Counterpoint, © 1983, reprinted by permission).

-32-

You gain strength, courage and confidence by every experience in which you really stop to look fear in the face. Do the thing you think you cannot do... do one thing every day that scares you.

Eleanor Roosevelt

I admire stories of courage. Can you imagine the courage of the Apollo 11 astronauts landing on the moon, facing the very real possibility of being stranded looking down at the earth 250,000 miles away with no way to return? (If your car battery dies outside the hardware store, it's one thing, but for them...).

No less inspiring are stories of everyday courage. I have had many patients like the man who was terrified to leave his home but summoned the courage to walk to the mailbox, then drive down the street, and then go to the grocery store. Or my neighbor who spoke to the unpopular opinion of supporting the school budget proposal—maintaining funding for music and creative arts—in our crowded town meeting.

Frederic C. Craigie, Jr., Ph.D.

Acceptance—looking challenges in the face—means looking beyond the suffering to see the possibility of a growth opportunity and sometimes, to recognize a message in disguise.

Emotions are a gift. They can be exhilarating. They can be painful. But often, they communicate something meaningful about where we could be going. We are, I believe, evolutionarily hard-wired to experience emotions, even if distressing, because they are useful in our survival and well-being. It's like acute pain. Acute pain is, well, a pain, but without pain, you wouldn't have the direct feedback that leaning on your thousand-degree woodstove is not a good idea.

The collection of experiences that we call "depression," for instance, often communicates "Your life is out of balance," "Maybe you need to make some changes," or "Maybe this is a time to back up a bit and think about where you're going."

The idea of emotions as messengers, of course, runs contrary to our cultural and medical/cultural assumptions. The health care culture, championed by the pharmaceutical industry, tells us that uncomfortable emotions are irredeemably bad and need to be done away with. We don't honor emotions enough.

Fear often communicates messages of "Be careful," or "Get away." Fear, hopefully, keeps you from going to close to the edge at Grand Canyon. Fear surely prompted soul-searching and planning for Austrian Jews in 1938 as they anticipated a knock on the door. Regrettably, the same is true for undocumented immigrants in America as I write this.

But it's more than that. Fear—in its everyday and particularly psychologically-grounded form, we use the word "anxiety"—communicates the message of "Here is

164

a growth opportunity." Anxiety points to choices we can courageously make that stand to expand our lives, to make our lives bigger and freer.

If you face the fear of driving and you drive, you expand your life. If you face the fear of public speaking and you venture to put yourself out there among other people, you expand your life. If you're anxious about telling someone that you love them and you do this, you expand your life. It is not a matter of doing any of these things flawlessly or comfortably; it is more a matter of developing the practice of listening to and honoring your feelings.

As Joseph Campbell famously commented, the cave that you are afraid to enter may just be the source of what you're looking for. You gain strength by looking fear and other uncomfortable emotions in the face. You expand your life by doing the things that scare you, the things you think you cannot do.

Reflection

- What do you think about the idea of uncomfortable emotions as messengers? Have there been times when you have felt anxious or demoralized and had the experience that these emotions pointed you in helpful directions?

- When have you "looked fear in the face" and made the choice to do what you were anxious about doing? What was this experience like; how did you feel about having done this?

- In the coming week, make a point to do something that scares you.

Frederic C. Craigie, Jr., Ph.D.

Author

Eleanor Roosevelt (1884-1962) was an activist and life-long advocate for progressive causes. She knew whereof she spoke about facing fear, emerging from her early years when, by all accounts, she was shy and lacking in confidence, to become one of the most prominent and admired women in the world.

She was born into a wealthy and politically-connected family (her uncle was Theodore Roosevelt) but suffered through a painful childhood. Her mother, her alcoholic father, and a brother all died before Eleanor was ten, and she was principally raised by a frequently-critical grandmother. Studying in London in her late teen years, she found a life-changing relationship with a mentor who helped her to become more independent and laid the groundwork for a passionate connection with the world of ideas and social causes.

Eleanor married Franklin Roosevelt in 1905, supporting him in his early political life while bearing and caring for four children. Learning of her husband's affair in 1918, she chose to remain married but was strengthened in her growing intention to create her own life and commitments.

In her years as First Lady, Eleanor found a platform to do this. She advocated for greater presence of women in government and in the administration, leading to the appointment of Frances Perkins, who was the impetus for many of the New Deal programs. She acted in solidarity with homeless coal miners and World War I veterans. She lobbied on behalf of African American rights and famously resigned her membership in the Daughters of the American Revolution when they denied the use of their principal venue to singer Marion Anderson. She held hundreds of press conferences and began a syndicated six-day-a-week newspaper column in which she discussed current events and humanitarian issues.

Nor did Roosevelt's activism slow down after her husband's death. Harry Truman appointed her as a delegate to the United Nations General Assembly, and soon after she became chair of the newly-formed United Nations Commission on Human Rights and was instrumental in developing the UN-sponsored Universal Declaration of Human Rights. She continued human rights advocacy in the remaining 15 years of her life, while she played an active role in Democratic politics, spoke out against McCarthyism, urged civil rights protections for African-American activists, chaired a commission on the status of women, continued her newspaper column, completed over two dozen books, and maintained a busy schedule of speaking around the world. You might join me in wondering if she ever slept.

The quotation comes from her 1960 *You Learn by Living: Eleven Keys to a More Fulfilling Life* (New York: Harper and Row).

Frederic C. Craigie, Jr., Ph.D.

GRATITUDE

Frederic C. Craigie, Jr., Ph.D.

-33-

[Let's] remember the great truth that moments of
surprise want to teach us; everything is gratuitous,
everything is a gift. The degree to which we are awake
to this truth is the measure of our gratefulness. And
gratefulness is the measure of our aliveness. Are we
not dead to whatever we take for granted? Surely to
be numb is to be dead. For those who awaken to life
through surprise, death lies behind, not ahead. To live
life open for surprise, in spite of all of the dying which
life implies, makes us even more alive.

David Steindl-Rast

Speaking at Columbia University Teachers' College in New York a couple of years ago, I took some extra time to be a tourist. Having known a sculptor who worked on the Cathedral of Saint John the Divine, this was one of my priority stops.

Like other Gothic cathedrals around the world, Saint John is immense and soaring and presents the visitor with a sense of mystery. Unlike many Gothic cathedrals, it is the

centerpiece of a thriving modern religious community and
has many elements of very current spiritual life.

Outside one of the chapels in the main sanctuary was
a several-foot-long white board with a supply of dry-erase
markers and the prompting question, "What do you treasure?" Filling all of the available space and overlapping with
one another, passers-by had written a colorful collection of
responses;

- Family and the gift of music
- My eyes
- Laughter
- My cats (Camille)
- The community my church provides for me
- My babies, all 45 of them
- Freedom, brotherhood, family
- Ability to choose careers
- This wonderful life we are fortunate to have
- Cookies
- The special plate given to me by my grandmother
- Carbs
- Going for a walk
- My dog is a blessing from God
- International friends
- Laughter, happiness, anger, sadness

What a wonderful and diverse list, from freedom and
brotherhood to cookies (the author of "carbs," I suspect,
might also treasure a wry sense of humor). And you can

imagine the stories that go along with these short entries. The 45 babies, the special plate, the dog—as they all are—a blessing from God.

The list speaks to gratefulness, and it captures the feeling of aliveness that gratefulness engenders. Can you feel the energy in some of these responses? Can you picture the people, young and old, as they were writing them?

To be awake to the blessings of your life brings you to life. A life absent of gratefulness—Steindl-Rast uses the words "numb" and "dead"—misses out on the richness and fullness of our humanity.

For all of us, there are surely some gifts of life for which we are constantly and eternally grateful. I wake up every morning, make some coffee, and have a modest time of reflection or meditation that always includes being thankful for the blessing that my wife has been in my life for all these years.

Surprise can be a special element of gratefulness, as well. Perhaps something calls to mind a blessing, like the special plate, that you don't much think about. Or perhaps you happen upon a new experience, like finding a whiteboard description of treasures in a Gothic cathedral, that makes you smile. To be open to surprise, to be awake to the blessings of life even in the midst of challenges and suffering, "makes us even more alive."

Reflection

- What would you write on the white board? What do you treasure?

- Invite into your attention some gift or blessing in life that's been there but you don't much think about.

- Recall a time when you were blessed by something that came to you as a surprise. An experience of wonder or awe. An unexpected encounter with someone. A moment that touched your heart.

- In the coming week, pause to express silent words of gratitude for blessings that are continuing parts of your life, and give thanks for unexpected experiences that touch your heart.

Author

David Steindl-Rast (b. 1926) is a Benedictine monk, writer, and social activist. He was born in Austria and drafted into the army during the Nazi occupation, but he escaped and remained successfully in hiding until the end of the war. He earned a doctorate degree in psychology in Vienna and then emigrated to the United States in the early 1950s, joining a monastic community in upstate New York. In the late 1960s, Brother David became actively engaged in interfaith dialogue, studying with Zen masters and co-founding the Center for Spiritual Studies, bringing together representatives of Jewish, Buddhist, Hindu, Sufi and Christian traditions. He is especially renowned for his promotion and celebration of the transformative role of gratefulness for individuals and for the broader society. In 2000, Brother David co-founded A Network for Grateful Living, which oversees the extraordinary website, www.gratefulness.org, providing resources and orchestrating community connections for people worldwide. For years, he has sought balance in his personal spiritual life, dividing his time between the reflective life of a hermit and the busy life of speaking and teaching internationally.

The quotation is from *Gratefulness, the Heart of Prayer* (Paulist Press, 1984).

-34-

Can you see the holiness in those things you take for granted--a paved road or a washing machine? If you concentrate on finding what is good in every situation, you will discover that your life will suddenly be filled with gratitude, a feeling that nurtures the soul.

Harold Kushner

Blessings abound. Some tap us on the shoulder or stare us in the face. Some, we take for granted.

I remember going with my dad when he bought his first brand-new car, a 1961 Dodge Lancer. He asked the salesman whether cars now all came with heaters. This was a serious question, and the man did not laugh. The answer was "yes" although cars did not come with radios and our AM radio receiver was an optional extra.

Now, we roll down the road in a cabin with all the comforts of home. Concert quality sound. Precise temperature control, whether it is raining, sleeting, or baking outside (adjustable for the tastes of driver and passenger separately, no less). Living in Maine for all these years, I confess that there have been times in the dead of winter when we'll get into the car and drive to no particular destination just to crank up the heat to 80 and have a respite from the cold.

And there's more, all around us. One-inch under-sea fiber optic cables carry data around the world with enough capacity for tens of millions of high-definition videos streaming simultaneously. Grocery shelves, at least in America, are never empty. Spring comes, and leaves unfold. In spite of notable exceptions (the media pays particular attention to this), most people are incredibly kind and generous.

Calling to our awareness the blessings that we take for granted is a spiritual practice. Kushner uses the word, "holiness." You will recall that our modern words *holy, health, heal,* and *whole* all derive from the Old English words, *hal/ halig.* There is considerable modern research demonstrating that gratefulness is associated with multiple aspects of well-being, including physical health, mental health, self-esteem and self-care, resilience, empathy, and sleep. But doesn't the awareness of blessings enliven us to the sacredness of life, as well? When you pause to recognize the gifts of life that you usually take for granted, doesn't that help you to transcend the circumstances of the moment and glimpse a larger view of the exquisite and holy tapestry of life?

Reflection

- Call to your attention five small blessings that you don't much think about, that you take for granted. Sit with your awareness of these blessings for a few minutes.

- Explore the idea of everyday blessings with the following exercise. Write down today's date on a piece of paper. In your mind's eye, project yourself forward to very nearly the end of your life. You are largely incapacitated; you are unable to do any of the things in your life that have brought you joy. Perhaps you are in discomfort. A kindly Presence appears and offers to return you, free of charge and with no strings attached, to your life as of today. You go for it, and you find yourself transformed back to being the person you are today. You can again move as you wish. You can do things that had been inaccessible in your state of near-death. Look around. In what ways do you experience yourself being blessed with today's life, in this context? Next to today's date, write down some parts of your life today for which you are grateful.

- In the week to come, open your awareness and your heart to some blessing each day which you might otherwise have taken for granted.

Author

Harold Kushner (b. 1935) is an American rabbi and internationally-prominent writer. He is best known for his books that explore suffering, forgiveness, and meaning-making, particularly the landmark *When Bad Things Happen to Good People* (Random House, 1981) and *When All You've Ever Wanted Isn't Enough* (Summit, 1986). His insights about the human condition have been formed by on-the-ground work as a congregational rabbi in the Boston area for over 30 years. Kushner is also no stranger to suffering himself, having lost his son Aaron to a rare disease in his early teens (prompting the question, "Where is God?" in his first book). Now approaching his mid-eighties, he is the recipient of six honorary doctorate degrees and a collection of awards touching on religious life and service. The quotation comes from Kushner's essay, "God's Fingerprints on the Soul," from a remarkable collection of

Frederic C. Craigie, Jr., Ph.D.

spiritually-inspired reflections in *Handbook for the Soul*, edited by Richard Carlson and Benjamin Shield (Little, Brown and Company, 1995).

-35-

The greatest thing is to give thanks for everything. He who has learned this knows what it means to live. He has penetrated the whole mystery of life: giving thanks for everything.

Albert Schweitzer

Gratefulness is not conditional. Gratefulness means being aware of and thankful for daily blessings, but thankfulness when things appear to be going well is just a slice of the pie. Gratefulness is a practice, an attitude, and a perspective on your life.

Even amid the trials and challenges of your life, isn't there a foundation—a big picture—for which you can be grateful? You are alive. If you're holding this book, you can see, and you can read. There is someone, somewhere, who loves you. You have the ability to choose who you are and who you are going to become. This is the reality, and it's always there in the background.

When families in 19th century America gathered for rare days off from work, they often went to cemeteries. In communities where the priority for land was that it should be productive, the most peaceful, serene and well-maintained public spaces were cemeteries. You could spread a blanket next to Great-Grandpa Hezekiah and Great-Grandma Prudence, break out the roast chicken, and have a grand time together.

Similarly, over the years, I brought lunch once or twice a month to a peaceful colonial-era cemetery a few minutes from the office. I'd enjoy the tranquility, sitting in my Volkswagen camper eating a sandwich, then often amble among the headstones.

What stories of joy and sadness! A man was "a kind husband, an affectionate friend, and very beneficent to the poor, the widow and the fatherless." A woman led a life that was "industrious, virtuous, religious, peaceable and charitable." But there are also many headstones recognizing people who died—children or young adults—far too young and whole families who passed away, presumably from infectious illnesses, in short succession. There are a few people, here in Maine, who were lost at sea. And there is the young man who died at Bull Run, and 20 feet away, another young man, presumably his small-town friend, who died at Gettysburg.

Perhaps in recognition of the fragility of life, early Americans often inscribed tombstones not with dates of birth but with age at death or, sometimes, with days lived. "Elizabeth Brooks, died October 20, 1758, aged 27 years, 8 months and 21 days." "Major Archibald Hoar, died January 31, 1782, aged 73 years, 5 months and 10 days."

Cemeteries give me a reverent reminder of the big picture of life, and along with the chicken and frivolity, I imagine this was true for our forebearers, as well. Headstones recognize people who lived short or long lives with much the same human experiences—laughter, loss, celebration, fear, love—that we experience. Some of them, I suspect, were insecure and shady characters, but many of them were stewards in the continuing flow of compassion and human caring across the generations.

Being "thankful for everything" means cultivating the spiritual practice of awareness of the big picture. You inherit a world that has been formed for you by countless people who have come before you. You are alive, and you are now the steward of those qualities of goodness that they have passed on.

This day is a gift. It provides an opportunity for you to bring to bear everything that you have learned up to this point in charting how you are going to live this unique and irreplaceable day. Is this not a cause for gratefulness?

Reflection

- Think of someone in your family or someone in your larger acquaintance outside your family who has taught you something about living a good life. Pause and give thanks for this person. Write him or her a note expressing your gratefulness, and if that person is still among us, send it.

- If it doesn't seem too maudlin, visit a local cemetery. Look around. Read some headstones. Even with modern markers that typically don't have inscriptions, notice the decorative images that people have chosen. Imagine what these people's lives may have been like and how they helped to form the world that you have inherited. What do you think they would have to say to you?

- How would you put into words what "the big picture" means for you—the reality, that's always there in the background, for which you can be grateful?

- In the week to come, pause a few times to sit in thankfulness for the big picture of your life.

Author

Albert Schweitzer (1875-1965) was among the most broadly-accomplished people of the 20th century, making major contributions as a theologian, musician and musicologist, physician, and peacemaker.

He was born in a small village in Alsace, then part of Germany, into a family of pastors, musicians, and scholars. Beginning music studies as a young child, he was a celebrated organist by his early teen years, and continued to perform to great acclaim for the rest of his life. He became a world expert on the interpretation of the organ music of Bach, publishing biographies of Bach in French and later in German. He was also interested in the technical aspects of the organ, studying and writing about organ design and building.

Schweitzer began theological studies at the age of 18, earning a doctorate degree and subsequently serving as a church pastor and as the administrator of the theological school from which he had graduated. In these years, he was particularly engaged in religious commentary, publishing his most noted theological work, *The Quest of the Historical Jesus*, in 1906 at the tender age of 31.

Not content to make noted contributions in two fields, Schweitzer began studies in medicine in 1905. At the completion of his training in 1913, he and his wife traveled to what was then French Equatorial Africa (now Gabon) to establish a hospital in Lambaréné. He was motivated, apparently, both by his awareness of the profound health needs of African people and as an expression of atonement for what he often publicly described as the abuses of colonialism. With the exception of a short internment during

Weekly Soul

the First World War and periodic international visits for concert performances and personal appearances (funds from which supported his medical work), he lived in Lambaréné for the rest of his life. I imagine this is the image that is most familiar to many of us about Schweitzer: the richly-mustached medical missionary administering a rural hospital and nimbly playing piano on the banks of the Ogooue River into his late eighties.

Schweitzer became involved in issues of nuclear proliferation in the last years of his life. He was awarded the Nobel Prize for Peace in 1952.

The quotation comes from *Thoughts for Our Times*, a short volume of edited quotations published in 1975 by Peter Pauper Press.

Frederic C. Craigie, Jr., Ph.D.

-36-

I have often been asked if people can—or even should—feel grateful under dire circumstances. My response is that not only will a grateful attitude help—it is essential. In fact, it is precisely under crisis conditions when we have the most to gain by a grateful perspective on life. In the face of demoralization, gratitude has the power to energize. In the face of brokenness, gratitude has the power to heal. In the face of despair, gratitude has the power to bring hope. In times of trial and tribulation, gratitude becomes our spiritual lifeline.

Robert Emmons

A mid-fifties colleague of mine was met with the recurrence of a cancer that had been diagnosed and treated several years before. When she first got the news, she was shocked, angry, and afraid, but within a few days, she regained a sense of equanimity and peacefulness. "It sounds cliché," she said, "but I'm coming to accept more of the moment, not to be greedy, to accept the gift I've been given. I practice a prayer of humility, being grateful for what I have, what I enjoy, what I'm blessed with, the air that I breathe."

185

"It helps me," she continued, "to be creative and conscious, not to go through life in a blur."

In perilous times, gratefulness can be life-giving. Gratefulness brings a different perspective and different energy to suffering. It opens our hearts to blessings, even in the face of pain. It is indeed hard to see the gift if your life is in a blur. When you are exclusively focused on suffering, there's not much room for what else may come your way.

Often, the gratefulness is *in* hard times, not necessarily *for* hard times. I do know people who have said that they were grateful *for* cancers and other serious circumstances—mainly because they learned to more fully savor the moments of their lives—but for most of us, it's more a matter of directing our attention and heart toward gratitude even *in* the midst of suffering. My colleague allowed herself to be angry, afraid, and confused, but recognized that she couldn't continue to live under the weight of these feelings. She needed to turn toward being grateful for ongoing blessings as a way of reorienting and restoring her life.

Life certainly can bring some terrible experiences that you wouldn't wish on your worst enemy: deaths of children, bitter divorces, and racial or ethnic discrimination. But the awfulness of these experiences is usually not the whole story. I have a long-time friend whose granddaughter died of a congenital anomaly at six days of age. In the midst of the tears, the salvation for this family was holding each other in the affirmation of what a "blessing" this young person had been to them all in her short life.

Clouds, after all, can have silver linings; the events that we summarily judge to be "bad" end up having blessings in disguise. I've heard from a number of students over the years—physicians, nurses and other caregivers—that their suffering as young people with serious illness opened doors to pursuing meaningful health careers because they were inspired by the kind and professional care that they received.

And, of course, silver linings can have clouds. There are the people who landed the perfect job, only to find that the boss was unbearably crotchety or that the culture of their new organizations just didn't align with their own values. You never know.

Gratefulness helps us to suspend judgment in painful circumstances. It orients us to the enduring and inalterable reality of who we are and what we care about, helping our attention to run deeper than the storm of emotions that usually attends suffering. It opens our hearts to new blessings along the way.

Reflection

- My suggestion to you is that gratefulness in hard times draws energy away from suffering and directs it toward blessings old and new. What is your reaction to this? Has this ever been your experience?

- Think of someone you know—a friend, an associate—who has had some "dire circumstance" and found their way to some measure of equanimity and peacefulness. How did they do this? Might gratefulness have been part of the journey for them? You can form your conclusions from afar or, of course, you can ask.

- In the coming days, notice times when life brings you some circumstances that you'd judge to be "bad" or unpleasant. Experiment with suspending judgment and reflecting on some reasons to be grateful.

Frederic C. Craigie, Jr., Ph.D.

Author

Robert A. Emmons, Ph.D. (b. 1958) is described by the Greater Good Science Center as "the world's leading scientific expert on gratitude." He serves as professor of psychology at the University of California, Davis where he has taught since 1988, and is the author of nearly 200 journal articles and book chapters, along with six acclaimed books for both scholarly and popular audiences. A leader in the positive psychology movement, Dr. Emmons is founding editor and editor-in-chief of *The Journal of Positive Psychology.* He is Past-President of the American Psychological Association's Division 36, The Psychology of Religion. His research focuses on the psychology of gratitude and thankfulness in both adults and youth and on the psychology and spirituality of joy and grace as they relate to human flourishing. Dr. Emmons has received research funding from the National Institute of Mental Health, the John M. Templeton Foundation, and the National Institute for Disability Research and Rehabilitation. His research has been featured in dozens of popular media outlets including the *New York Times, USA Today, U.S. News and World Report, Newsweek, Time, NPR, PBS, Consumer Reports, Reader's Digest,* the *Wall Street Journal,* and the *Today Show.*

The essay from which this quotation comes is published through the website, *DailyGood,* and may be seen at http://www.dailygood.org/story/532/how-gratitude-can-help-you-through-hard-times-robert-emmons/.

FORGIVENESS

Frederic C. Craigie, Jr., Ph.D.

-37-

Forgiveness is capable of producing some of the most profound transformations you could ever hope for or imagine in your life and the lives of others. Forgiveness can change everything – overnight. That's what's so exciting about it. It can change everything. It can bring joy where there is sorrow, peace where there is turmoil, gladness where there is anger. And it can give you back to yourself.

Neale Donald Walsch

Dr. Everett Worthington had been a professor of psychology at Virginia Commonwealth University for many years, specializing in the study of forgiveness and developing a case for the benefits of forgiveness for physical health, mental health, relationships, and spiritual life. Then, on New Year's Eve 1996, he received an anguished phone call from his brother, Mike. Mike had come upon the body of their mother, Frances, who had been brutally killed in a home invasion. It was, police said, a gruesome scene.

Adding to the horror that anyone would experience at this terrible loss was the background that Worthington's research and writing had made him a national expert in the process of forgiveness. Can you imagine a harder challenge of practicing what you preach?

His initial reaction was furious. If he were in the room with the killer, he said, he would have beat out his brains with a baseball bat.

Over time, however, Worthington became increasingly unsettled by seeing this vengeful reaction in himself. He made the decision to forgive the killer. "Chains fell off," he reflected. "A weight was lifted off my shoulders. I felt free."

Asked if this decision dishonored his mother, he said that to the contrary, his forgiveness of the killer honored his mother because it was what she would have wanted. She had taught him that virtue would be tested and that testing would reveal how much a virtue is embedded in one's life.

Sadly, the journey was different for Mike, who was never able to make peace with the image of discovering the murder; he committed suicide several years later.

In the setting of woundedness, forgiveness gives you back to yourself. It frees you to live your life, forever carrying with you the memory of a wound or a loss but no longer allowing it the power to hold you captive. You live your life directed and empowered by who you choose to be, not surrendering control to past events that aren't going to change.

Forgiveness is not absolution. It does not offer a blank check to allow abusers to continue to abuse. It is not an indication of weakness. It is not necessarily reconciliation.

It is also not shallow. As I've heard this story many times, I have been relieved to hear about the baseball bat comment, the initial feelings of fury and retribution. Everett Worthington— "Ev," to those of us who have been privileged to work with him—is a gentle, soft-spoken, peaceable

Tennessean. I have a hard time picturing him dispatching a catfish caught in a backwater pond. If he can have feelings like that, maybe the rest of us can, too.

But he recognized that you can't stay there. Bitterness and vengefulness corrode the soul. You have probably heard the widely-quoted proverb, attributed to Confucius and others, "Before you embark on a journey of revenge, dig two graves."

As I speak with people about forgiveness, the idea of choosing to forgo revenge often provides a turning point in reclaiming one's life in the wake of woundedness or loss. The modern word *forgive*, in fact, has its origins in the Old English/Old Saxon *fargeban*, "to give up desire or power to punish." And so, a woman who had been the victim of sexual abuse commented, "I realized I couldn't keep focused on revenge with this man; I had to let that go. And it occurred to me that the best revenge would be living a good life."

Whatever else forgiveness may eventually mean, it can start with a decision, a commitment, not to exact retribution. Even if victimizers are beyond the possibility of actual revenge—far away, inaccessible or dead—it's a choice to move your attention and heart away from the desire for revenge: choosing not to perpetuate a cycle of hate and abuse and focusing, instead, on living a good life.

Reflection

- What does forgiveness mean to you?

- When have you found yourself feeling bitter about unfair or abusive treatment from someone else? What was your initial reaction? Did your response change at some point? Does this perhaps remain an issue for you?

- In the week to come, notice any times when you feel mistreated. Think about what you might do so that this experience doesn't capture your spirit and keep you from being who you are.

- If you are interested in exploring the subject of forgiveness, I would also strongly commend the Martin Doblmeier film, *The Power of Forgiveness*. It is a remarkable, thought-provoking documentary that combines expert commentary (from Dr. Worthington, along with Elie Wiesel, Thich Nhat Hahn, Thomas Moore and others) with powerful human stories of woundedness and forgiveness. Available online in DVD format.

Author

Neale Donald Walsh (b. 1943) is an American writer and speaker. He engaged in several occupations before a series of untoward events (a consuming house fire, a divorce, and a motor vehicle accident in which he sustained a broken neck) left him destitute in the early 1990s. At a particularly low point, he awakened in the middle of the night, reaching out to God and was aware of a voice that he understood as The Divine, giving him instruction about what it takes "to make life work." This began a long series of encounters—he describes himself as a "spiritual messenger"—that formed the basis of his *Conversations with God* series of best-selling books.

The quotation is from Walsch's preface to Gerald Jampolsky's book, *Forgiveness, the Greatest Healer of All* (Hillsboro, OR: Beyond Words Publishing, 1999).

-38-

Forgiveness is something freely granted, whether earned or deserved; something lovingly offered without thought of acknowledgment or return... it makes us one with the human family and allows us to live in the sunlight of the present, not the darkness of the past. Forgiveness alone, of all our human actions, opens up the world to the miracle of infinite possibility. And that, perhaps, is the closest we can come, in our humble human fashion, to the divine act of bestowing grace.

Kent Nerburn

"My dad was like Jekyll and Hyde, without very much of the nice Hyde part." An early-60s financial services professional told her story. "He put up an OK front on the outside—he had jobs most of the time and we had a house—but inside the house, it was really different. Especially when he was drinking, he was abusive and cruel. He never left a mark, but he'd shove me around and would yell at me and tell me that I was stupid and would never amount to anything. He'd lock me in my room. He'd say he wished he'd had a son instead of me. I spent a lot of my childhood feeling terrified, and I guess my mom felt that way, too."

"As soon as I was 18," she continued, "I was out the door, and years would go by without my even laying eyes on him. Then four or five years ago, I took a course on forgiveness at my church and thought of him. The question, I think, was 'Who in your life have you most hardened your heart against?' Somehow, I got the idea of visiting him. I found out from my brother that he was in a nursing home an hour or so away and made the trip."

"When I went in, he was sitting by himself at one corner of the dayroom. I was struck by what a thin, frail-looking man he was; I remembered him as a big, hulking ogre. He was, of course, surprised to see me, and we chatted for a few minutes. What do you say after all those years? I told him it looked like he needed a friend and asked if it would be OK for me to come back. He brightened a little and said that would be nice."

"On the way home, I thought about my life and thought about his life. I remember hearing from my mom that he had been beaten all the time by an alcoholic father when he was growing up so maybe that's what he knew. I visited him a couple more times without daring to speak the word, *forgiveness*, and we talked about more and more sensitive things. Then, I knew what I had to do. I told him that we couldn't undo the pain from all those years, but that I wanted now to forgive him and love him. He didn't have words but stood up and gave me a hug, with tears rolling down his cheeks. The next six or eight months before he died were a real blessing to be with the father that I finally had."

The base model of forgiveness involves a commitment to forgo revenge and retribution such that taking energy away from past abuses frees us to live our lives.

The LX model of forgiveness comes with additional features. Sometimes, forgiveness opens up the possibility of renewed relationships with other people.

Forgiveness, in this form, is an altruistic act, as Nerburn says, "freely granted" and "lovingly offered." It often begins with seeing unforgiving people in a different light. The woman in our story recognized that her father had himself been a victim and that his life experiences had pushed him in the direction of becoming the person he was. She came to see him as a fundamentally lonely and unhappy man, which he may well have been for many years before she connected with him toward the end of his life. Her decision of forgiveness, as she said, was to tell him that the history of abuse couldn't be undone but that she was willing to love him and see where their relationship might go.

Does this altruistic forgiveness excuse abusive behavior? Of course not. Is a reconciled relationship easy sailing? Often, no. Does a renewed relationship with people make you vulnerable to renewed abuse? Maybe, maybe not.

What altruistic forgiveness does is to open our hearts a little bit, as we see people doing the best they can with what they've been given, as we see them being more than their abusive acts, and as we glimpse the shared humanity of navigating the hills and turns of life. And it offers the possibility of a meaningful connection with people who we have frozen out of our lives. At its best, this is sacred. This is grace.

Reflection

- What is your experience with the "LX model" of forgiveness? (The reference, by the way, is to my 1999 Honda Accord, which was a great car until it rusted out after too many Maine winters.) Have you had the experience of reaching out in a spirit of grace to someone whom you have frozen out of your life, or has someone perhaps reached out in this way to you?

- What do you picture the woman in our story having done if her father had refused her altruistic forgiveness? Might her commitment of forgiveness still have been meaningful for her even if their relationship wasn't going to go anywhere?

- In the coming week, experiment with a meditation of lovingkindness. Sit quietly, and hold this intention for yourself:

May I be safe!

May I be happy!

May I be at peace!

Then hold this intention for someone whom you love:

May (name) be safe!

May (name) be happy!

May (name) be at peace!

Then, hold this intention for someone out there to whom you have no emotional connection, like a grocery store clerk.

Then, finally, hold this intention for someone with whom you have a troubled relationship. Experience love, altruistically given, moving toward and enfolding this person.

Weekly Soul

Author

Kent Nerburn (b.1946) is an American artist and writer. Growing up outside of Minneapolis, he was inspired to a life of service as he followed his father, the Midwest director of disaster relief for the American Red Cross, to all of the calamities that drew police and firefighters. It gave him, he says, an understanding of suffering. He earned a Ph.D. in Religious Studies and Art and devoted a number of years to creating large sculptures carved from tree trunks, expressing themes of harmony with nature and peace. He worked with and became immersed in the culture and sacred traditions of the Ojibwe community in northern Minnesota, interviewing and documenting the oral histories of tribal elders. In his early forties, Nerburn redirected his creative journey from visual arts to writing, beginning a succession of books that explore the intersections of indigenous spirituality, the Judeo-Cristian tradition, and the natural world. The quotation comes from *Make Me an Instrument of Your Peace: Living in the Spirit of the Prayer of St. Francis* (HarperOne, 1999).

Frederic C. Craigie, Jr., Ph.D.

-39-

Forgiveness is essential in life because we make mistakes all the time. Sometimes we're put in impossible situations where people get hurt even when we're doing the right thing; a boss who has to fire an employee who is undermining morale, for instance, or a mother who has to stop giving money to her drug-addicted son. How do we forgive ourselves when we cause others pain, knowingly or unknowingly? The first step is to keep our hearts open to our own remorse rather than deflect it with anger or self-justification. Then we respond compassionately with ourselves, in words or deeds.

Christopher Germer

A nurse in her early 30s described a painful and emotionally wayward background, during which she had flirted with substance abuse and had a series of relationships with needy and clinging people. As she was getting her life together, she reflected,

> It has to start with loving myself, accepting myself in spite of the poor decisions I have made, because if I don't love myself, then I just allow myself to get

drawn into bad relationships and if I love myself, then that frees me to be who I am.

Indeed, we make mistakes all the time: errors of commission and errors of omission. I cringe when I think of all the times I have spoken something unkind or thoughtless, when I have held back from being engaged with something that really needed my attention, when I didn't know what to do, or when I flat-out made wrong decisions. Times, looking back, when I might have acted with greater kindness, wisdom, courage, or circumspection in my personal life and in my professional life.

Mistakes and failures are part of the human condition. Forgiveness frees us of the corrosive effects of these shortcomings. It frees us to learn and grow. It changes our relationships with ourselves.

There are challenges, of course. Forgiving ourselves is not always easy. For most of us—most of you reading this—it's a lot easier to be charitable with other people than it is to be charitable with ourselves. It's cultural, at least in the circles where I travel, that it is harder to accept and love ourselves than it is to accept and love other people. Being judgmental with ourselves, unfortunately, can be a badge of honor.

Forgiveness and compassion for ourselves are intertwined with self-care. Unforgiveness drains away the energy for self-care. I have lost count of the students, colleagues, and friends who have conflated self-acceptance and time spent on self-care with selfishness.

Against the background factors that weigh against it, self-forgiveness is a vital life skill and practice. Forgiving ourselves—loving ourselves and caring for ourselves in spite of mistakes and failures—benefits our health and well-being. It reclaims control of our lives from the emotions of past events that won't change. It is self-affirming, not selfish. And it frees us to change and grow.

What, after all, is the alternative? Does self-condemnation or self-deprecation help? After some consideration, the answer that most people come to is "no." People may say that they deserve a measure of punishment or denial for their mistakes or offenses. Perhaps this is sometimes appropriate, but how much is enough? Is there a statute of limitations? Or people may say that self-denigration makes it more likely that they will be accountable in the future. I'm all for accountability—you can't blithely make the same mistakes over and over—but self-forgiveness *fosters* accountability more than it impedes it. As Carl Rogers famously commented, "The curious paradox is that when I accept myself as I am, then I can change."

If self-condemnation doesn't help, then you need to find a Plan B, right? Often, a good starting point for self-forgiveness is to reflect on what someone who dearly loves you would say to you about your shortcomings or offenses. Think of someone who knows you well and dearly loves you. It may be a particular person in your life—a partner, a parent, a grandparent who has passed on, a best friend—or it may be a revered spiritual or religious figure or Presence: Jesus, the Buddha, Mother Teresa, Desmond Tutu, the Great Spirit. As you and they look together at your shortcomings, what would they say to you? What would they tell you? Can you then treat yourself in the same way that they would treat you? Might it, in fact, dishonor them for you to treat yourself any differently?

Reflection

- We have all been critical of ourselves, for many good reasons, but there is a difference between bottomless self-deprecation and looking earnestly at our

Frederic C. Craigie, Jr., Ph.D.

mistakes and then turning toward self-forgiveness. When have you experienced—allowed—this transition in yourself? What effects of this new perspective have you seen?

- Is there perhaps some particular event in your life now where you have hardened your heart against yourself? What do you think keeps you there? Can you imagine turning more toward gentleness and compassion with yourself with this?

- And now, a longer exercise that I often share with groups. There are two steps of preparation. First, invite into your attention some mistake, shortcoming, or failure on your part that remains a challenge for you. Second, find words that describe how you would like to relate to yourself about this. Be creative; these are your words. Past examples have included:

  - Be gentle with myself.
  - Love and accept myself.
  - See that the good in me far outweighs the bad.
  - Be kind toward myself.
  - Give myself permission to treat myself kindly.
  - Forgive myself.
  - Treat myself as my grandmother would treat me.
  - Embrace all of who I am, today.

Now put these together as a meditative exercise:

  - Even though (call clearly to your attention the event you're working with) ...

- May I (insert words of forgiveness or affirmation) ...
- So that I can live my life.

Sit with this for a few minutes.

- In the week to come, notice the times when you are regretful and self-critical, and see how you might treat yourself with these events in a life-affirming way.

Author

Christopher Germer, Ph.D. is a Boston-based clinical psychologist and educator. His particular interest is in mindfulness and self-compassion. Early on, Germer's travels and studies in India helped to inspire a career-long exploration of the benefits of mindfulness and meditative practices. In 2008, he began a collaboration with Kristin Neff, Ph.D., focusing their work together on the development of the Mindful Self-Compassion (MSC) program. The program has been taught to over 100,000 people and is being researched and adapted for specialized populations. Together, Germer and Neff have written two books on MSC and have established the Center for Mindful Self-Compassion (centerformsc.org), which supports teachers and practitioners of MSC around the world. Germer is also a founder of the Center for Mindfulness and Compassion at the Cambridge Health Alliance, (chacmc.org). The quotation comes from Germer's book; the title of which will not surprise you, *The Mindful Path to Self-Compassion* (Guilford, 2009).

Frederic C. Craigie, Jr., Ph.D.

-40-

When you set out to change the world, the job seems insurmountable. But each of us can do his or her small part to effect change. We change the world when we choose to create a world of forgiveness in our own heart and minds. It is our nature to forgive, to reconcile and rebuild the broken pieces of our relationships. Every hand that extends itself in a gesture of forgiveness is a hand working toward the creation of peace in the world.

Desmond Tutu

On the clear, moonlight night of November 14, 1940, nearly 500 Nazi bombers took off from bases in occupied France and flew to the British industrial city of Coventry. In the first attempt in history to destroy an entire city in a single attack, they dropped 500 tons of high explosives and forty thousand firebombs. The toll was enormous, with the loss of several hundred lives and 60,000 buildings. Beholding the destruction of the irreplaceable 12th century cathedral the following morning, the cathedral provost, Richard Howard, went to a still-standing wall and inscribed in chalk the words, "FATHER FORGIVE."

The remainder of the war, sadly, witnessed unabated acts of retribution, including the infamous 1945 allied firebombing destruction of Dresden, a militarily insignificant German city, at a cost of 35,000 civilian lives. However, in the years to come, the provost's intention urging the Coventry community to banish thoughts of revenge set in motion a process of forgiveness, reconciliation, and partnership with other international cities, Dresden among them, that had suffered the same fate. Today, Coventry University hosts a Centre for Trust, Peace, and Social Relations that orchestrates research and community projects arising from the legacy of forgiveness and reconciliation around the world.

Forgiveness changes individuals, and forgiveness changes the world.

Revenge, among communities, is perpetuated in an endless cycle as much as it is with individual people. Forgiveness holds the power to bring the destructive flow of retribution to an end and open the possibility of new life where there had before been darkness and death.

Tutu, himself, was at the forefront of healing the collective trauma of generations of violent apartheid in South Africa. How, he and others asked, do you heal a society that has seen countless acts of unspeakable violence and brutality for years and years? The solution, they found, lay in community forgiveness built upon a structure of truth and reconciliation. Individuals would choose to come forward, often in the presence of victims or families of victims, and forthrightly describe what they had done. Having spoken this truth, they would be invited to be part of a society of new relationships.

The process, Tutu has said, has its origins in the South African concept of *ubuntu*, the understanding that we are all participants together in shared humanity, and that fractures in our relationships with one another must be repaired in order for any of us to be made whole. In South Africa, the TRC process helped to avert a bloodbath of retribution at the end of apartheid, and the same process has now been employed in dozens of similarly-fractured communities and nations around the world.

Forgiveness changes individual human hearts, and by the cumulative ripple effect of people and communities following the courageous path of forgiveness, it changes the world.

Reflection

- When have you seen forgiveness played out beyond your personal, individual experience? Have you ever, in some way, been part of a community initiative of forgiveness? Has there ever been a story of someone else's expression of forgiveness that has touched your heart and inspired you to think about your own experience?

- A colleague of mine was on one of the World Trade Center airplanes on 9/11, and I recall feeling anger and grief about his death and about the unspeakable inhumanity of the day. Having said that, what do you imagine—for better or for worse—may have been the unfolding of events in the following years if we had collectively chosen Richard Howard's response of "Father, Forgive?"

- In the week to come, take some time to sit with Tutu's assertion that "every hand that extends itself in a gesture of forgiveness is a hand working toward the creation of peace in the world."

Frederic C. Craigie, Jr., Ph.D.

Author

Desmond Tutu (b. 1931) is a renowned South African theologian and social activist. Growing up during the British colonial era, he graduated from the University of South Africa and taught briefly as a high school teacher before beginning theological studies. He was ordained into the Anglican priesthood in 1960.

Tutu's career in the church took him to a succession of appointments as an educator, administrator, and inter-denominational leader. He has served as Bishop of Johannesburg and as Archbishop of Cape Town, in both cases being the first black person to occupy those positions. He also was chosen to lead the South African Council of Churches, and later, the All Africa Conference of Churches, using the platform of these roles as a prominent public advocate of racial justice.

With Nelson Mandela's release from prison and subsequent election as president of South Africa, he invited Tutu to chair the Truth and Reconciliation Commission to investigate past human rights abuses during the apartheid years. With intensive and emotionally charged dialogue over the course of two years, the commission navigated a process of confession, forgiveness and restitution to help to work toward national healing and reconciliation.

Throughout his career and into this century, Tutu has been a forceful advocate of peace and justice issues. He has stood in support of the ordination of women, of gay rights, of HIV/AIDS treatment and of economic and social liberation of oppressed minorities around the world. He vocally opposed the Iraq war. Tutu was awarded the Nobel Peace prize in 1984.

Recently, Tutu collaborated with his long-time editor Douglas Abrams in publishing a book that distills wisdom from five days of conversation with Tutu and His Holiness the Dalai Lama. *The Book of Joy* (Avery/Random House, 2016) is a charming, intimate, and deeply-moving reflection on how to "find joy in the face of life's inevitable suffering."

Our quotation comes from Tutu's book, written with his daughter Mpho, *The Book of Forgiving* (HarperOne, 2014).

Frederic C. Craigie, Jr., Ph.D.

CREATIVITY

Frederic C. Craigie, Jr., Ph.D.

-41-

The effort to bring something new and meaningful into the world – whether in the arts, the kitchen or the marketplace—is exactly what generates the sense of meaning and fulfillment for which so many of us yearn so deeply.

Peter Korn

In the range of 65,000 years ago, someone wandered into a network of caves in what is now Spain, finding a suitable wall surface and inscribing images of animals and geometric designs. In ever-unfolding fields of archaeology and cultural anthropology, these images presently claim title to being the oldest examples of visual arts yet discovered. They were made by Neanderthals, long before modern humans appeared on the scene, giving rise to fresh theories about the sophistication of what we have long considered to be barrel-chested, dim-witted brutes.

In the following millennia, people around the world left behind increasingly elaborate cave art, culminating in the richly-colored and energetic human and animal images in Lascaux. In my seasonal home in Arizona, progenitors of today's Native American communities created above-ground rock art—animal forms, hand prints, sun images, spirals and the omnipresent flute player named Kokopel-li—relatively recently in the timeline of human life but still thousands of years ago.

Theories abound about what lies behind images like these. Perhaps they were created in gratefulness or celebration of a community accomplishment like a successful hunt, or in petition for successes to come. Perhaps they marked the cycles of life. Kokopelli, for instance, symbolizes fertility in addition to music. Perhaps they had some spiritual significance not yet understood.

Whatever their origin or meaning, these ancient images are art. They are creation. The coincidence of these images with such a long scope of human history attests to me that it is fundamental to our nature, as Korn says, "to bring something new and meaningful into the world."

Creativity matters. The data show that creativity enhances brain function and basic physiological health and supports a range of physical and mental health outcomes. But it's more than that. When you bring something new into the world—painting, photography, music, dancing, writing, cooking—you bring new energy into your life. The energy and spirit inside of you have a chance to meet the light of day.

Creativity moves in different ways. Sometimes the creative process is fairly well marked from the beginning, as in "Now I'm going to write a poem about social justice," or "Now I'm going to try to capture this stunning Maine seascape in watercolor." Sometimes, you really don't know where you're going, and it emerges. The process takes on a life of its own. My friends who are novelists say that their characters often chart their own lives in the writing and surprise their authors with what they say or do. Sometimes, the creative process draws upon and evokes emotions that defy being limited by words. When I compose a fiddle tune, it's much more about the feeling and movement of the music than it is about language and ideas.

However it emerges, the fruit of your creativity out there in the world can touch other people. I imagine that you, like me, have had the experience of being moved to tears by a piece of music that brings you back to a memorable episode in your life. And who among us has not been moved by a painting that draws you in, or an expressive dance routine, or by a poem that touches your soul?

Ultimately, though, the creative process is personal. You don't create for the audience... or even if you create something with a loving, gifting destination, it has to pass muster with your own heart first. If no one ever sees your cave painting, or reads your poem, or hears your music, you can take satisfaction in having given life to something that never existed before. Something that arises uniquely from you. Empowering "the sense of meaning and fulfillment for which so many of us yearn so deeply."

Reflection

- I refer above to "painting, photography, music, dancing, writing, cooking." These are among a larger list of creative arts. What is your experience with the creative arts? How has your exploration or expression of creativity added something personally meaningful for you?

- How would you put into words where your own creativity comes from? Do you find that there are times when you have been more productively creative, or that you have ever done something to lay the groundwork for the creative process?

Frederic C. Craigie, Jr., Ph.D.

- If you had the time and resources, what form of creative art might you wish to explore?

- In the coming week, create something new—a doodle, a tune, a few words of poetry, a new recipe of your own design. It does not have to be extraordinary; in fact, it's likely to be more meaningful if what you create is purposefully not ready for prime time. How does this feel?

Author

Peter Korn (b. 1951) is a furniture maker, designer, writer, and educator. Coming of age in the late 1960s and early 1970s, he embraced the ethos of many young people at the time, aiming to craft a life that would be simpler and more fulfilling than that of their parents' generation. He completed his college degree at the University of Pennsylvania and bypassed his father's hopes that he would pursue a professional career, heading to Nantucket to work as a carpenter and home builder. This was his first experience of working with his hands, and he found it both difficult and immensely satisfying. He began to design and build furniture—finding the craft of woodworking very different from carpentry—and developed his skills, his business, and a network of fellow artisans over a number of years. Korn began writing about the process of furniture making, publishing his first book, *Working with Wood: The Basics of Craftsmanship*, in 1993. Increasingly, he became intrigued with the "why" of furniture making, along with the "how" of furniture making. He founded an institute on the coast of Maine that invites visitors to explore the craft of furniture-making art, both the techniques and the philosophy around bringing things "new and meaningful into the world."

The quotation comes from *Why We Make Things and Why it Matters: The Education of a Craftsman* (David R. Godine, 2013).

Frederic C. Craigie, Jr., Ph.D.

-42-

We fail to use our powers when we fail to think of our lives and our work, whatever it is, as creative—as potential art, or "life art."

Dan Wakefield

Creativity applies to all of life, not just the Arts.

Wakefield goes on to give examples of a telephone operator singing greetings in answering the phone, of a business person seeing the possibilities of a new product, and of a yoga teacher's creative guided meditation. This was the mid-1990s. I'm frankly not sure whether there are telephone operators anymore, but you get the idea.

It is, as Wakefield says, "life art." You have the ability to choose how you do what you do and to make even mundane daily activities into exercises in creativity.

You can explore a different process of interaction in your committee meetings. You can tinker with your choices in clothing. You can try something new with the kale and red peppers that are left in the fridge. You can move the furniture that's been in the same place for ten years, or paint the living room a different color. You can make up some bedtime stories for your 6-year-old daughter. You can pack the dog in the car and go with him to a new walk or take him on the regular walk and try to see it with new eyes.

When I was growing up, my father would find great joy in planning family motor trips around the country. Long before the days of GPS and Internet research, he'd study maps and tourist brochures and lay out an itinerary to get to the high spots of wherever we were going: a site rich in history, a national park, a music, or theater venue. He had a particular passion for anything related to railroads: rolling stock, museums, excursion lines. Planning distances, I remember, was based on the premise that you could count on 45 mph on US highways and 60 mph on the newly-developed Interstate highways.

All of this is creative. It's all art.

The same benefits attend life art as attend art in the narrower sense. There is the inherent satisfaction of doing something new, of bringing a new and creative way of doing what you do into the world. You take something ordinary and infuse it... bless it... with your soul.

But for art both in the broad and narrow senses, there is another benefit. You learn. You grow. You shed some of the old skin and try out a new one. I remember the comment of a poet I interviewed many years ago, "I write to learn something about myself." Indeed. And I believe the same is true for composing a song, proposing a new program at your town meeting (which is the way we do things in rural Maine), or dying your hair a color that isn't found in nature.

There is something powerful in living out your creative instincts. Putting yourself out there. Putting ideas into words. My experience is that when I want to understand something more clearly in my life or work, I write. Or I develop a teaching session, whether or not it really takes place. Creatively getting out ideas and seeing how they may or may not come together usually brings me, eventually, to a sharper understanding of the way things work.

What you are reading is Exhibit A. I began with my belief that creativity is an essential dimension of life well-lived and warranted equal billing among the dozen-or-so other chapters of this book. Then began the creative work. What do I know and what can I say about creativity, anyway? What does the literature say? What is my experience? What have I learned from my life and from what I have seen in the lives of other people? How might I succinctly describe the key elements of the creative process, and what stories could give life to the conceptual bones? I sit with the quotations. I make an outline. I try out some words. I take it again from the top and see what I'm missing or what could be expressed more clearly.

You enrich your life when you create art. And you enrich your life when you stretch yourself in some new and creative ways, seeing the whole canvas of your life as art, as well.

Reflection

- Think of a couple of times when you have done something new and creative in the spirit of "life art." Sit with your recollection of what this was like for you, or perhaps you may wish to write a few words of reflection to yourself.

- What thoughts occur to you about how you might "stretch yourself in some new and creative ways?" What might interfere with your pursuing such things? Obstacles vary, by the way. For planning and building a deck on the back of your house or re-doing your kitchen, the challenge is probably one of time and resources. For dying your hair the color that isn't found in nature, the challenge is more likely emotional. For whatever new and creative pursuits you're considering, how will you find your way around the barriers that could stand in your way?

- In the coming week, experiment with one or two ways of creatively stretching yourself that are logistically within your reach.

Author

Dan Wakefield (b. 1932) is an American writer and, for many years, an educator of writers. His own writing has been remarkably diverse, publishing essays in national magazines such as the *New York Times Magazine* and the *Atlantic Monthly*, publishing five novels and eleven books of nonfiction, and writing screenplays for movies and television. As an educator, he has taught in writing programs around the country, most recently retiring after 16 years as Writer in Residence at Florida International University in 2010.

Wakefield's work is particularly infused with his passion for the life of the spirit, writing and presenting workshops internationally on developing the spiritual autobiography and on spirituality and creativity. The quotation was originally published in Wakefield's 1996 book, *Creating from the Spirit*. The book was republished as the edition that I have used, titled *Releasing the Creative Spirit* (Skylight Paths, 2001).

-43-

Just don't give up trying to do what you really want to do. Where there's love and inspiration, I don't think you can go wrong.

Ella Fitzgerald

Ella Fitzgerald, the "Queen of Song," had a legendary career that spanned over half a century. Beginning in the early 1930s, she performed with the likes of Dizzy Gillespie, Benny Goodman, Nat King Cole, and Frank Sinatra and helped to form new styles in American popular music. She was noted both for her vocal and artistic range and for her remarkable improvisational ability. Reacting to the formulaic style of big band swing music, Fitzgerald was at the cutting edge of bebop, the jazz movement that turned away from prominent bass lines and featured extended improvisational solos from instruments like saxophone and clarinet or from the voice in the role of instruments. You can go to the Internet and see clips of her scat singing: singing nonsense syllables in tandem with other musicians as they together react to one another's melodic lines and chord changes.

Her formula for her creative work? Love and inspiration.

Inspiration goes by different names. It is a close cousin to "intuition." It is sought after by creative artists in its incarnation as the Muse.

The word comes from the Latin *inspirare*, to "blow into" or "breathe upon," especially, as the word evolved, in the sense of breathing life or spirit into people's experience. In-spiriting. Spirit moves, spirit flows, as the wellspring of creativity.

Where, you ask, does it move *from?* How do you invite the creative spirit or charm the Muse into appearing? For better or worse, there is an astounding amount of research and writing about creativity, without any consistent answers to such questions.

Some people find their ways to remarkable creative expression in the midst of troubled emotions and suffering. Think Van Gogh. Or F. Scott Fitzgerald (presumably no relation), who wrestled with alcoholism and depression even as he wrote *The Great Gatsby* and *The Beautiful and the Damned.* J. K. Rowling, author of the Harry Potter series, memorialized her own emotional struggles in the creation of the dementors, dark creatures that feed on human happiness and suck the life out of their victims.

Some people find creative expression in the setting of anger or as an outgrowth of trauma or injustice. Picasso's monumental canvas, *Guernica*, was a response to fascism and to the brutality and despair of the Spanish Civil War. Leonard Bernstein famously arranged a stunning performance of Gustav Mahler's Second Symphony, the *Resurrection*, two days after the John Kennedy assassination, saying "This will be our reply to violence: to make music more intensely, more beautifully, more devotedly than ever before."

My own experience is more pedestrian: jogging. When I'm not paying attention to the passing scenery, I find that the repetitive motion of running (biking does this, too) provides fertile ground for creative ideas. Or sitting on the front porch drinking coffee at the beginning of the day. Or, as you know, putting words to paper.

In my research, largely with physicians and other health care providers, I consistently hear that the ability to be present and to think clearly and creatively with patients rests on a foundation of spiritual groundedness. Our spiritual groundedness helps us to be more open to the wellspring of wisdom and intuition that surrounds us. As one family doctor commented, "When I'm really centered, when I can let go of all of the ideas and emotions that keep me from being present, that's when I'm most open to the inspiration of God's voice."

It's individual. It's personal. The wisdom and the experiences that form the creative spirit in you are yours to explore and yours to cultivate.

There is, as well, a place for love. It's hard to be creative if you don't love what you do. It's hard to persevere through the dry spells if you don't love what you do. And if you find a sustained lack of inspiration and creativity with something, you might give some thought to why you're doing it.

Reflection

- Inspiration—in-spiriting—was a vital part of Ella Fitzgerald's creative work. What is your experience with inspiration, or intuition? Think of a time when an idea, insight, or creative innovation has come to you: the solution to a problem, a fresh perspective, or a new direction. How, do you think, did this come to be? Is the process by which this came to life something that you can learn from or reproduce?

- Who is out there, whose creativity you admire? What do you know—or what might you find out—about the process of their creative inspiration?

- Particularly for visual artists, writers, actors and musicians, there is often a lineage of creativity, a succession of teachers and mentors who inspired them and helped them with the emergence of their own voice. Pay attention to what people say about their mentors and why they were important to them. You can look, for instance, at jacket liners of music, acknowledgments in books, and performance notes in theater.

- There is no lack of ideas about exercises or practices to invite inspiration. Read Julia Cameron. Put pen to paper and write freely for ten minutes. Listen to music that touches your soul and then jot down some reactions.

- In the week to come, be attentive to times when you experience some inspiration or intuition. Write a few words about what happened and what you think created the conditions for it to come to life.

Author

Ella Fitzgerald (1917-1996) grew up in modest surroundings north of New York City, part of a supportive family and community. Her happy childhood years were met with loss and trauma in her early teens. Her mother died from injuries sustained in a motor vehicle accident, and not long afterward, her stepfather died from a heart attack. She fell off in her school work and had minor brushes with the law, resulting in a short and abusive placement in reform school. In later years, she said that the emotions of this time in her life helped to fuel the energy that she brought to her artistic work.

Weekly Soul

Fitzgerald had her first break in music when she sang, to great acclaim, at an Amateur Night event at the Apollo Theater in Harlem in 1934. This set in motion a succession of musical contacts and partnerships in Harlem—a dynamic center of the world of innovative music—and beyond. Over the long course of her career, she toured internationally, made regular guest appearances on television, won 13 Grammy awards, and sold over 40 million albums. In 1987, she was awarded the National Medal of Arts by Ronald Reagan, and in 1992, the Presidential Medal of Freedom by George H. W. Bush.

Frederic C. Craigie, Jr., Ph.D.

-44-

If you don't live it, it won't come out of your horn.

Charlie Parker

In the 1976 movie, *Eleanor and Franklin,* there is a remarkable scene with actress Jane Alexander in the role of Eleanor. It's 1918, and Franklin has just returned from a trip to Europe to inspect naval facilities. In among the luggage that Franklin brought back with him, Eleanor discovers a packet of love letters from Lucy Mercer, her social secretary, with whom Franklin has been having an affair. The camera holds uncompromisingly on Alexander's face as her expression changes from curiosity to anguish as she reads the content of the letters. She is distraught. She cries.

As a psychologist, I don't lack for experience with people crying, but this is an actress, portraying somebody else's life. Crying is largely involuntary. How, as she plays this scene, does Alexander allow tears to flow? A friend of mine who is herself an actress says, "She connects with the grief that's there in her own life. To be in a role like that, you have to draw from real life."

Frederic C. Craigie, Jr., Ph.D.

Creative expression has genuineness… has integrity… when it flows from real life. As Parker says, you have to live it.

I'm sure this is not news to anyone who is involved in the Arts. I remember reading comments from the legendary dancer and choreographer Martha Graham; becoming a mature dancer, she said, is a twofold process. The first part consists of honing the body musculature and developing technique. The second part, often after some years of training, consists of cultivating the being of the artist. Dancers learn to infuse their work with their life experience, their feelings, and their passions— "the legends of the soul's journey…"—in making for rich and powerful creative expression.

So it is, as well, for those of us who are not specifically engaged in the Arts. Any act of creative expression— teaching a high school class, writing a sympathy card, talking politics with your neighbor over the back fence—will have greater energy and authenticity if it is grounded in your own life experience.

I see this in myself in presenting talks and workshops. In years past, when I've given presentations that dutifully summarize and extrapolate from professional research literature, it's been academically responsible but not especially engaging. I still aim to be academically responsible, but what I share with people is now much more rooted in my own observations and life experience. What do I really *know* about integrative health and resilience in health care providers (a topic that is dear to me)? How do I know what I know? What stories have I heard that touch my heart? What have been formative events in my own life that inform what I believe? And how can I invite people to share from their own life experience in ways that teach and enliven us all?

Conversations that are grounded in questions like these have energy. Authenticity. Life.

Creative expression is a fundamental part of human nature. It is part of the journey and part of the joy of being alive. It pertains to the Arts, and to all of life. It is fueled by in-spiriting, which comes to us along many different pathways. And it finds energy and authenticity as it draws on the wellspring of real life.

Reflection

- Think of the perennial second-level security option for most website access; "Who was your favorite teacher?" What was it about this person that was important and memorable for you? As I speak with people, the common responses that I hear include:

  - He was creative in his teaching.

  - She inspired me.

  - He was passionate about the subject.

  - She wasn't just doing a job; she was a real person.

  Do these responses line up with your experience? Do you see a pattern here? Where do you think the energy and inspiration for their creative teaching came from?

- At this point in my life, most of my early teachers are probably quite elderly, if indeed they are still among us at all. If you are young or fortunate enough that your favorite teachers are, as a patient once said, "on the right side of the grass," talk with them. Correspond with them. Ask them how they came into their own creative and inspiring spirit.

- What about you? The premise here is that your creative expression will be more energetic and authentic as it draws on your own life experience. You have to live it to have it come out of your horn. It's not the book learning; it's not just the technical skill. It's what you really *know* from your own life. Can you think of times when your own creative approach to your work, to your relationships and interactions, or to your approach to some challenge or problem was energized in this way?

- In the coming week, pause to look at your own creativity, in creative arts or in your life more broadly, and think about how your own life experience informs this expression.

Author

Charlie ("Bird") Parker (1920-1955) was a celebrated American saxophonist and jazz musician. The beginning of his musical odyssey was in grade school. His mother had given him his first saxophone, and he played in the school band. He became enthralled with the instrument and left school at age 15 to pursue a musical career. During this period of his life, he later recalled, he spent three or four years practicing 15 hours a day. (Think of this as you consider your own experience with piano lessons.) Parker began performing and then recording professionally, collaborating with all of the prominent jazz musicians of his era. He is known both for his virtuosity and for his singular creative vision for his music, breaking new ground with chord progressions, rhythms, and solo improvisational styles not seen before in jazz. With Dizzy Gillespie, he was the principal originator of bebop. His personal life was marked with struggles with substance abuse and mental health issues, and he died at age thirty-four.

Parker's quotation is reported in *Bird: The Legend of Charlie Parker* by Robert Reisner (Da Capo, 1977). The full quotation cited is, "Music is your own experience, your own thoughts, your wisdom. If you don't live it, it won't come out of your horn. They teach you there's a boundary line to music. But, man, there's no boundary line to art."

Frederic C. Craigie, Jr., Ph.D.

CIVILITY

Frederic C. Craigie, Jr., Ph.D.

-45-

Hate for hate only intensifies the existence of hate and evil in the universe. If I hit you and you hit me and I hit you back and you hit me back... that goes on ad infinitum. It just never ends. Somewhere somebody must have a little sense, and that's the strong person. The strong person is the person who can cut off the chain of hate, the chain of evil... Somebody must have religion enough and morality enough to cut it off and inject within the very structure of the universe that strong and powerful element of love.

Martin Luther King, Jr.

Civility is vital to a good life.

We will all, sometimes, be faced with difficult people. Difficulty, of course, is not a singular or inalterable character trait, but you know what I mean: people who treat you or others in ways you consider unfair, people who are just a little too full of themselves, and people who see the world and follow paths that are profoundly and disturbingly different from yours.

Frederic C. Craigie, Jr., Ph.D.

How do you react to someone whom you experience as consistently condescending or critical? How do you relate to your next-door neighbor, who is proudly and vocally at the other end of the political spectrum from you? What do you do as you notice in yourself a welling-up of anger or, dare I say, hate?

These are important and timely questions. A number of factors in recent years have made for dramatic increases in social polarization and incivility, which population data show to be significant public health issues. Like unforgiveness, incivility haunts the beholder without improving the landscape at all.

Experiencing the loss of a dear friend, Donna Red Wing wanted to do something that would honor her friend and the values that had marked her life. Her friend was, she said, "all about reconciliation and reaching out to people." So, Red Wing considered "who would be the most unlikely person on the planet I could reach out to?" The executive director of Iowa's largest lesbian, gay, bisexual, and transgender organization, Red Wing chose Bob Vander Plaats. Vander Plaats was the executive director and CEO of The Family Leader, an evangelical Christian organization that had forcefully advocated for conservative perspectives on sexual identity and expression.

Donna invited Bob (they refer to one another with first names) to coffee. With some trepidation on both sides, they met and began to test the waters about getting to know one another. Over several conversations, they discovered that they had a lot in common. They realized that in spite of their opposing social views, they could respect each other and, indeed, had come to like each other. Neither of their fundamental perspectives had changed, but the tone of how they would represent those perspectives had changed.

"We can fight the good fight," Donna says, "but we don't have to hurt each other, because if we hurt each other, we're hurting ourselves." "If Bob and I can have coffee," she continues, "if we can laugh and tell stories to get to know one another, if we can like each other, then I think that almost anyone can find that person in their life and reach out and find that they can like each other."

Civility means fighting the good fight—advocating forcefully for ideas that matter to you—but doing it in a way that respects the human dignity of someone else: not buying in to stereotypes or assumptions about other people, being willing to take some even-hesitant steps to reach out to the person you experience as difficult, listening, and committing not to return hate for hate. Civility does double duty. It saves your soul and usually makes the world a little more peaceful and habitable in the process.

Reflection

- King closes this thought with the phrase, "that strong and powerful element of love." Love, of course, was at the heart of King's writing and of his public life. As you think about how you relate to the difficult people in your life, what does "love" mean to you? How does this fit in?

- What particularly pushes your buttons with other people? Perhaps when you experience people as being unfairly critical? Arrogant? Selfish? Deceptive? Or perhaps holding social or political positions that are anathema to you? When has there been a time when you have related civilly to people that you find difficult? How did you do this?

- We've been looking at civility in the context of relationships with people whom you've met or may stand to meet. How do these ideas pertain to your feelings about people whom you are likely never to meet? How does the outward and inward practice of civility apply, for instance, to public or political figures whose behavior is disturbing for you?

- In the week to come, identify someone you experience as "difficult." Think about what it would look like to relate to this person in thoughts and action in a spirit of civility.

Author

The Rev. Dr. Martin Luther King, Jr. (1929-1968) is a person who, indeed, doesn't need much introduction. Born into an educated and comfortable African-American family in Atlanta (his father was a celebrated preacher and activist), King graduated from Morehouse College, completed seminary in Pennsylvania, and attained a doctorate in theology at Boston University. He rose to prominence with his leadership of the Montgomery bus boycott, which was prompted by Rosa Parks' civil disobedience and concluded with a Supreme Court case striking down racial segregation in public transportation. He was at the forefront of civil rights activism for the rest of his life, co-founding and chairing the Southern Christian Leadership Conference and leading campaigns in Birmingham, Selma and elsewhere in both the South and North on behalf of voting rights, open housing, and social change. He delivered his iconic *I Have a Dream* speech at the March on Washington in 1963, with some of the most powerful phrases being a departure from his prepared text at the urging of Mahalia Jackson, who told him, "Tell them about the Dream."

King ran afoul of many supporters, both black and white, with his opposition to the Vietnam War, which he saw as a neo-colonial expression of American economic interests at the expense of poor people in both the United States and Vietnam. Inspired by the social consciousness in the life and writings of Gandhi, he considered resistance to civil injustice and to economic injustice to be two sides of the same coin. King was awarded the Nobel Peace prize in 1964.

King's public ministry came at great cost, leading to his assassination in 1968. His house was bombed, he suffered a near-fatal attack in 1958, and he was jailed over two dozen times. One of his incarcerations provided the impetus for his 1963 *Letter from Birmingham Jail*, making the case for nonviolent resistance to racism.

The quotation comes from King's sermon, *Loving your Enemies,* delivered on November 17, 1957, at the Dexter Avenue Baptist Church, in Montgomery, Alabama.

You can see features about the relationship of Donna Red Wing and Bob Vander Plaats by entering their names into the YouTube search bar.

Frederic C. Craigie, Jr., Ph.D.

-46-

Understanding and love are not two things, but just one.
When you understand, you cannot help but love. You
cannot get angry. To develop understanding, you have
to practice looking at all living beings with the eyes of
compassion. When you understand, you love. And when
you love, you naturally act in a way that can relieve the
suffering of people.

Thich Nhat Hanh

As a young African-American boy growing up in pre-dominantly white Boston suburb, Daryl Davis knew little of racism. As he moved along into his middle school years, though, incidents began to come up that showed him the dark reality of racial discrimination even in his comfortable northern community. His experiences prompted a life-long question, "How can you hate me when you don't even know me?"

As an adult, Davis became a professional musician, performing boogie woogie and rock-and-roll piano around the United States and internationally. His musical life provided an unforeseen opportunity to begin to address his question.

In a break during a set in Baltimore, a white man approached him, saying that he had never heard a black man "play like Jerry Lee Lewis" and offering to buy him a drink. They sat down together, talking about music, and the white man observed that this was the first time he'd had a real conversation with a black man. "Why," Davis asked? Because the white man was the grand dragon of the Maryland Ku Klux Klan!

This set in motion a remarkable odyssey for Davis into the world of the KKK. From the Maryland man, he obtained contact information for Roger Kelly, then the Imperial Wizard, the national leader, of the KKK, and set up a meeting with him. Unaware that Davis was black, Kelly arrived with an armed bodyguard, and he and Davis began an awkward and tentative conversation. Initially, it was largely one-sided, with Davis asking Kelly about his beliefs and experiences and listening attentively to the answers. Gradually, in this and later meetings, it became more two-sided, with Kelly asking Davis about his experiences, as well. They met, at first, at neutral sites. Then, Davis invited Kelly to his home. Eventually, Kelly invited Davis to his home. At Kelly's invitation, Davis attended KKK rallies, abhorring the values they represented but respectfully curious about what would make people choose such a path. Both Kelly and Davis being prominent in their own rights, CNN sent a crew to investigate. Why would a black man go to a KKK rally? As you may expect, this made for head-shaking national news.

Kelly and Davis came to respect each other. They considered each other to be friends. Coming to know Davis, Kelly's views about African-Americans softened, and he ultimately chose to leave the Klan, giving Davis his KKK robe as a token of respect and gratitude.

To date, over 200 people have left the KKK because of Davis' influence, and he has assembled a warehouse worth of Klan robes as a testament to their changed lives. A substantial relief of suffering, indeed! Along with his musical gigs, Davis now speaks widely about understanding and transformation.

The work of civility is fueled by compassion. Compassion often grows as we take some tentative steps to understand other people. Who is this person? What is it like to be them? What life experiences have brought them to where they are? Where is there a back story of suffering? Understanding, often, softens our hearts about the people we find difficult.

I remember supervising a resident physician in our primary care practice who was caring for a middle-aged diabetic woman. She would come in month after month, grossly overweight, her blood sugars far out of control. She didn't exercise. She had a terrible diet. Medically, nothing changed. The resident would roll his eyes when he saw her listed on his schedule.

We talked about exploring the back story of this person's life. Who is she? What is it like to live her life? It turned out that she was absolutely devoted to caring for two little grandchildren who had been largely abandoned by their parents. As she spoke about this, you could see a very different spirit in her eyes. The resident's heart—as mine—softened, and he was able to form a more positive, collaborative relationship with his patient going forward.

The challenge with people we find difficult is that it is easy and tempting to rest in the story that's on the surface: the annoying behavior, the outlandish public positions. The temptation is to see people as adversaries—sometimes, as enemies—who are fundamentally and irrevocably flawed. But other people are the way they are for reasons, and looking for the back story of those reasons can make for a step toward civility. "When you are calm, when you are lucid," Thich Nhat Hanh goes on to say, "you will see that the other person is a victim of confusion, of hate, of violence transmitted by society, by parents, by friends, by the environment." When you see that, your heart softens.

Organizational consultant Margaret Wheatley says it well, quoting the proverb that "You can't hate anyone whose story you know."

Reflection

- My phrase that you have now read several times is "soften your heart." Roger Kelly's view of Daryl Davis was softened as was Davis' view of Kelly and as was the resident's view of his diabetic patient. Thich Nhat Hanh speaks of love. Eyes of compassion help you to understand other people, and understanding nurtures love. What do you think about this?

- Thich Nhat Hanh also pronounces a remarkable end point. Civility is fine. Respectful dialogue is fine. Not returning hate for hate is fine. All of these end points surely move us toward a more peaceful and grace-filled world. But his end point is different: the relief of someone else's suffering. This, he suggests, is both an honorable way to live your life and a perspective that frees you from the anguish of needing interpersonal outcomes that work in your own self-interest. Can you imagine yourself approaching difficult people with the hope to relieve their suffering? Have you done this?

- Can you really not hate anyone whose story you know?

- In the week to come, choose someone whom you find difficult. With eyes of compassion, look for the back story. What can you find out about the larger picture of this person's life? What experiences may they have had that brought them to where they are? Where, perhaps, is there suffering? Might this exploration change in some way how you feel about them?

Author

Thich Nhat Hanh (b. 1926) is a Vietnamese monk, scholar, peace activist, and, well… enlightened soul. Often referred to in Vietnam as *Thầy*, ("teacher," "master"), he was born in the central region of what was then French Indochina and followed a path of Buddhist education from an early age. He was ordained as a monk in 1951 and was largely devoted in the 1950s in the movement to nurture Vietnamese Buddhism and in the outreach to develop rural infrastructure such as schools and health clinics.

As the Vietnam War approached, Nhat Hanh charted a course that combined personal spiritual discipline with service to people who were being displaced by the fighting. He described this as "Engaged Buddhism," the bringing-together of inner transformation and social activism.

In the 1960s, Nhat Hanh traveled between his native Vietnam and the United States, teaching at Princeton and Columbia, founding Van Hanh Buddhist University in Saigon, and speaking on behalf of non-violent peace initiatives. In a 1966 trip to the United States, he met Martin Luther King, Jr. and urged him to publicly declare opposition to the war. Growing out of this relationship, King delivered his sermon, *Beyond Vietnam: A Time to Break Silence*, at the Riverside Church in New York City. Later that year, King publicly announced that he had nominated Nhat Hanh for the Nobel Peace Prize. Such a public pronouncement was contrary to the protocol of Nobel prizes, and no peace prize was awarded that year.

Nhat Hanh continued his activism as chair of the Vietnamese Buddhist peace delegation to the Paris peace talks. As a result of his peace initiatives, both North and South Vietnam denied him permission to return to his home country, ultimately resulting in an exile of 39 years.

In the years since the war, Nhat Hanh has had an active life of teaching and writing. He has published over 100 books, the majority of them in English. In 1982, he founded Plum Village in southwest France, a community that has become the largest Buddhist monastery in the West and has hosted tens of thousands of seekers after the art of mindful and peaceful living. He has also established monasteries in the United States, Europe and around the world, and spoken widely to governmental and non-governmental organizations about ending the cycles of violence, war, and global warming.

When we in the United States think of Nhat Hanh, what often comes to mind is his emphasis on mindfulness. Contrary to the narrow way in which mindfulness is sometimes understood, it is important to underscore Nhat Hanh's perspective that mindfulness is not fundamentally a tool or technique that would be used to procure something else, be it health, serenity or material success. Rather, his view is that mindfulness extends to the whole of one's life, in peaceful and harmonious relationships with oneself, with others, and with the natural world.

The Thich Nhat Hanh quotation comes from *Being Peace* (Parallax, 2005). Margaret Wheatley's reference to the proverb about hate comes from her book, *Turning to One Another: Simple Conversations to Restore Hope to the Future* (Berrett-Koehler, 2009).

-47-

In the school of life, difficult people are the faculty. They teach us our most important spiritual lessons, the lessons that we would be most unlikely to learn on our own.

Mark I. Rosen

Civility has outer work and inner work. The outer work, if not easy, is at least straightforward. You listen to people. You give them a chance to speak. You communicate that you're enough interested in understanding them that you're willing to hold off on coming at them with your own opinions or rejoinders. You allow the possibility of a seedling relationship to grow.

The inner work can be more challenging. How are you going to position your heart so that you are able to reach out in civility to someone who feels like the enemy? The outer work of civility takes place in the realm of behavior; the inner work takes place in the realm of attitudes, beliefs and perspectives.

Some attitudes and perspectives make it very difficult to engage with somebody in a civil way. If you buy in to the

Frederic C. Craigie, Jr., Ph.D.

premise that a difficult person is thoroughly evil, culpable, and deserves to suffer (and let's be honest, these thoughts go through your head, too, yes?), then you really can't be curious about their life in any believable way.

Other perspectives open the door to the outward work of civility, at least a crack. For MLK, it was the reminder that returning hate for hate "only intensifies the existence of hate and evil in the universe." For Thich Nhat Hanh, it is the belief that the people we experience as difficult are often suffering themselves, as victims of misunderstanding, cruelty or abuse. For Donna Red Wing, Bob Vander Plaats, and Daryl Davis, it is the conviction that looking for the shared humanity in somebody else holds the potential to transform walled relationships.

Mark Rosen adds an additional perspective to the inner work of civility. Difficult people are our teachers.

Jacki (you've read enough of these stories to recognize that's not the real name, right?) is a mid-forties woman who has a painful traumatic background. She was sexually abused as a child and again in her first job when she moved away after college. Neither of the perpetrators was either accountable or repentant. In the case of the adult rape, Jacki's allegation became public, without any resolution. The abuser was a prominent person in the community and had a reputation for local generosity and benevolence such that the criticism and shame fell much more to Jacki than to him.

Jacki says that these experiences have made her the person that she is. She has had lessons about unmerited suffering that she otherwise would never have had. She has learned to be resilient in the face of criticism. She has come to recognize that she always has choices in how she responds to life events. "I can choose to wallow in self-pity or I can become who I'm meant to be." And she has decided that advocating for and supporting other women who have had similar experiences will be a central part of her own life journey going forward.

Although she has no interest in any relationship with the adult abuser, Jacki sees this person occasionally in the community and is able to interact with him in a civil way. "Every time I see him," she says, "I remind myself that I wouldn't be the person I am without him and that I can make the whole thing less about him and more about what I've learned and what I'm continuing to learn."

Seeing difficult people as teachers allows us to step back from the emotions of the moment. It moves our experiences and reactions into a larger landscape. It offers the possibility of opening up some new lessons in how we're going to live our lives.

Reflection

- What is your experience in learning from difficult people in your life? Think of a particular person. Even though your experience with this person may have been unpleasant, how would you put into words some way in which this person has helped you to become the person that you are?

- From a spiritual standpoint, as I suggest, civility pertains both to outward behavior and to the inner life that undergirds it. How do you think that your inner life of thoughts, assumptions and beliefs affects your ability to be civil in your outward life?

- Jacki doesn't use the word forgiveness. Is what she is describing, in fact, forgiveness? Or is forgiveness in some way different?

- In the coming week, notice someone whom you experience as difficult. Think of this person as the faculty in your school of life. What might he or she be there to teach you?

Author

Mark I. Rosen, Ph.D. is an expert on organizational life and behavior, presently serving as associate professor in the Hornstein Jewish Professional Leadership Program at Brandeis University. His research and teaching have particularly focused on leadership and management in Jewish nonprofits, and on elements of Jewish life in families and communities. The quotation comes from his 1998 book, *Thank You for Being Such a Pain* (Three Rivers Press). A scholarly man with an apparently robust sense of humor.

-48-

Love is inside us, just waiting to be unleashed. The darkness is an invitation to light, calling forth the spirit in all of us. Every problem implies a question: Are you ready to embody what you say you believe? Can you reach within yourself for enough clarity, strength, forgiveness, serenity, love, patience and faith to turn this around? That's the spiritual meaning of every situation; not what happens to us, but what we do with what happens to us and who we decide to become because of what happens to us.

Marianne Williamson

I have a remarkable colleague, Julie M Bosch, Ph.D., ARNP, who was deployed twice to Afghanistan as a Lt Col nurse practitioner. Her role was both clinical and educational, caring for casualties of war and teaching nursing skills to Afghan staff. She came to realize that her teaching was less about clinical procedures and more about modeling and affirming human presence and compassionate care. "I learned," she said, "that the language of nursing care and compassion is universal. I didn't need an interpreter most days as I could tell the level of pain by looking at my patients' faces. I learned it came down to the basics: sitting down, listening, caring, being present."

Julie's commitment to present and compassionate care would be put to the test. Her first deployment took her frequently "outside the wire," leaving the relative safety of the base to travel to outlying hospitals in a Humvee as part of a convoy. She carried loaded sidearms at all times—incongruous and awkward for a nurse—in the ultimate contingency of protecting her patients as mandated by the Geneva Convention.

Julie arrived at a hospital one day to find several patients who had just been admitted. She could sense disdain and revulsion on the part of the Afghan nurses, who were refusing to take care of them. They were, she was told, Taliban fighters who had been seriously wounded when bombs they had been setting for her convoy had exploded prematurely.

She faced a stark choice. What do you do when your professional work challenges you to care for someone who has been trying to kill you? She tells the story:

> The Afghan nurses didn't want to take care of them. Apparently, these guys were the enemy. I didn't pretend to understand the politics of it all. To me, they were patients. They wore hospital gowns. They had long unruly beards and wild black hair that stuck out all over their heads. They were not large men, not the monstrous visions I had in my head. They looked poor and a little lost and scared. They had intravenous lines in their arms, urinary catheters attached to their bodies that drained yellow urine, their blood was red, they had grievous injuries from their wounds—

they were wounded humans. They weren't my enemy. They were my patients.

It was what I saw in their eyes that gave me pause.
I saw fear. I saw darkness. It was also suspicion
and—hate. I still just saw a patient. I just saw a human. I had been a nurse for nearly 30 years. Being
a nurse was my identity. It defined me in this scary
place. If I turned away or refused to take care of
them, I would have been lost. I would have lost
my identity, my sense of my own self. I would never have been able to find my way home, in every
sense of the word. Everything I needed to know I
saw in their eyes. The rest was easy.

Do not give difficult people the power to keep you
from being who you are. The choice that Julie faced was
clear. She could follow a path of retribution by keeping
her distance and ignoring the suffering of these men who
had had such heinous intentions toward her. Or she could
be faithful to her calling as a nurse. Her decision was that
these men were not going to have the power to keep her
from honoring her fundamental and overarching commitment to care for suffering.

Julie's story frames the idea of "difficult people" about
as starkly as you can imagine, but the lesson is played out
in lesser ways every day. Can you respond to unfair criticism without being punitive? Can you respond to sarcasm
without becoming sarcastic yourself? Can you resist the
temptation to jump wholeheartedly with your friends into
a chorus of snide and self-righteous remarks about another
person whose behavior falls somewhere between annoying
and reprehensible? Can you, indeed, reach within yourself

to find and draw upon the goodness and integrity of who you really are?

The idea of holding true to your own values and identity touches on both the inner and outer work of civility. The inner work means recognizing the overarching values that make you who you are. The outer work means honoring those values in relating to people whom you find difficult. You can be direct and forthright with both your perspectives and your emotions. But civility means living in ways that hold the possibility of bringing a little more compassion and community into the world that so desperately needs both.

Reflection

- Think more about the inner and outer work of civility as remaining faithful and steadfast to the overarching reality of who you are. Look at this from two angles. When has there been a time when you have allowed yourself to be drawn in to reacting to a difficult person in ways that don't honor the values that are important to you? How did this feel? When has there been a time when you have been steadfast in being the person you want to be, even when the temptation or social pressure was pulling you in a different direction? How did that feel?

- I mention the temptation of joining with your friends in a "chorus of snide and self-righteous remarks" about other people. Any of us who are less pure than Mother Teresa probably do joke about other people from time to time (as I imagine they do about us). But it's a slippery slope. It is easy to get caught up in joining with like-minded friends in getting some laughs by vilifying somebody else. Where is the line drawn, where good-natured ribbing becomes toxic?

Where is the line drawn where earnest criticism of somebody else becomes personally demeaning and vindictive? Are you able to recognize when you are in danger of crossing these lines?

- Create a mantra for your own use for times when you are challenged to stay faithful to your own values in the face of mistreatment from people you find difficult. Six or seven words. "When I am faced with people whose behavior I find difficult, I will not give them the power to make me respond in ways that dishonor who I am. Instead, I will (mantra)"

- In the week to come, cultivate civility by noticing how you are able to hold fast to values that are important to you in the face of difficult people.

Author

Marianne Williamson (b. 1952) is an American writer and social activist. She has had countless names applied to her life and work, some with affection and some—especially as she has been publicly engaged in the political world—with derision. Apparently, she particularly chafes at the term, *New Age guru*, and her preference is to be called simply an *author*.

Williamson's early adult years were marked by a series of troubles with relationships, substances, and mental health issues. In the mid-1970s, she happened upon *A Course in Miracles*, a non-religious, nonsectarian program of spiritual life and growth centered around universal human themes of love and forgiveness. After some initial reservations, she began studying and then speaking about the Course with great enthusiasm, and its tenets have informed her life and service since that time.

Frederic C. Craigie, Jr., Ph.D.

While maintaining her own work of writing and speaking, Williamson has been active in a number of arenas of community development. She has chartered programs supporting people affected by HIV/AIDS, promoting national and international peace initiatives, and providing leadership training for women in politics. Williamson, herself, ran unsuccessfully as an independent for Congress in California in 1994 and for president in the 2020 cycle. She participated in the first two Democratic presidential debates, giving voice to some positions that had been little addressed in her party, such as moving the health care debate toward the social and environmental conditions that make people sick, resolving college debt, exploring reparations for the legacy of racial injustice, and frankly drawing upon the force of love in political discourse.

Williamson is the author of over a dozen books, many of them best-sellers, including *The Gift of Change: Spiritual Guidance for a Radically New Life* (HarperSanFrancisco, 2004), from which the quotation comes.

HOPE

Frederic C. Craigie, Jr., Ph.D.

-49-

To be hopeful in bad times is not just foolishly romantic. It is based on the fact that human history is a history not only of cruelty, but also of compassion, sacrifice, courage, kindness. What we choose to emphasize in this complex history will determine our lives. If we see only the worst, it destroys our capacity to do something. If we remember those times and places—and there are so many—where people have behaved magnificently, this gives us the energy to act, and at least the possibility of sending this spinning top of a world in a different direction. And if we do act, in however small a way, we don't have to wait for some grand utopian future. The future is an infinite succession of presents, and to live now as we think human beings should live, in defiance of all that is bad around us, is itself a marvelous victory.

Howard Zinn

The Democratic Republic of Congo is considered the worst place in the world to be a woman. Years of brutal civil conflict and economic exploitation have created a culture in which rape, torture, and trafficking of women and girls is widespread. Estimates are that as many as half a million rapes have occurred since the beginning of what is known as the First Congo War in 1996, with the perpetrators—both armed militias and members of state forces—almost never held accountable. Victims are often shamed and ostracized by their families and communities.

In 2007, Congolese gynecologist Dr. Denis Mukwege invited American playwright and activist Eve Ensler to visit his hospital to witness the massive human tragedy that he had been facing. They partnered with Belgian/Congolese human rights activist Christine Schuler Deschryver in founding a transformational healing community for victims of sexual violence. They named it "City of Joy."

A powerful 2016 film, *City of Joy,* traces the beginnings of the community and the experiences of the first group of women to live there. They come distraught, with stories of unspeakable violence and abuse. Many suffer debilitating physical sequelae of their abuse, and almost all suffer traumatic emotional reactions. They are welcomed and met with kindness. They embark on a multi-faceted 6-month journey of story-telling, emotional release and training in practical life skills from meal planning to self-defense. Notably, the women are not treated as pitiable victims who need to be saved, but as resilient women who can learn to chart their own courses of healing and claim an awareness of power that they likely had never experienced before. There is much anger, and there are many tears. There is also laughter. Women come to know and trust one another. Gradually, a spirit of community forms, and there is a blossoming of joy.

To date, City of Joy has graduated over a thousand women. They go back to their communities as social workers, teachers, and directors of schools, journalists, and radio hosts, and as emissaries to other women and girls with the lessons that they have learned about love, community and healing. Together with Iraqi human rights activist Nadia Murad, Dr. Mukwege was awarded the 2018 Nobel Peace Prize.

Hope... hoping... includes the recognition that the narratives of demoralization and despair that so often fill the news do not represent the whole picture. There is often a remarkable, inspiring reverse side of the coin.

In his 2018 book, *Enlightenment Now*, Harvard cognitive psychologist Steven Pinker presents data showing that major indices of health and well-being of the world are much better than they have ever previously been. Life expectancy, infant mortality, famine deaths, extreme poverty, major wars, homicides, literacy, occupational deaths—the list goes on—have all moved in favorable directions, in many cases, substantially in the last 50 years. In my own small corner of the world, I have often pointed out to medical residents, students and colleagues that chronic post-traumatic stress is actually less common that post-traumatic growth, and that it is important to look for, honor and be supportive of both.

These data and observations do not diminish the tragedy and injustice that remain and probably will always remain. But we need to recognize that along with darkness in the world, there is light. Along with cruelty, there is goodness. Along with suffering, there is healing.

Hearing hopeful narratives matters. American folk singer and activist Pete Seeger once commented, "The key to the future of the world is finding the optimistic stories and letting them be known." Indeed. Optimistic stories— the narratives of hope—hold and provide very different energy from the narratives of despair. As Howard Zinn says, that energy gives us the power to act.

Frederic C. Craigie, Jr., Ph.D.

Reflection

- As you look at the world out there, what optimistic stories do you see? Where do you find hope?

- Remember that stories have power. Sit with a particular hopeful story or narrative that comes to mind. Picture the rich details of this story: the people, the colors, the sound, the movement. What feelings or reactions do you see in yourself as you experience this story?

- In the coming days, be attentive to the optimistic, hopeful stories that you see in the larger world or in your own part of it. Stories of light in the midst of darkness, goodness in the midst of cruelty, or healing in the face of suffering.

Author

Howard Zinn (1922-2010) was an American university professor, writer, and social activist. He grew up in Brooklyn, the child of Jewish immigrants who both worked menial jobs to support their family during the Depression. Having no books in the home and seeing their son's interest in reading, they sent ten cents a month to the New York Post to purchase each of 20 volumes of the collected works of Charles Dickins.

As a young man, Zinn crossed paths with other young people in his neighborhood who were interested in communist ideas as an alternative to the economic disparity that they saw around them. He attended a rally in Times Square in which the peaceful marchers were charged by mounted police. Zinn was knocked unconscious. He reflected in later years that this event was a turning point in his life, persuading him that he could no longer trust in the benevolent intent of government and that radical social change was necessary.

After high school, he worked as an apprentice shipfitter in the Brooklyn Navy Yard, helping to found a workers' cooperative of apprentices, since workers at his level were ineligible for regular union membership. This experience began a lifetime of involvement and support for union movements.

Concerned about the spread of fascism, Zinn volunteered for the Army Air Corps at the outset of the second world war. He served as a bombardier on B-17s and competed missions throughout Europe. As the war was winding down, he was involved in a bombing run in southwestern France in which napalm was dropped on a small city that by that point had no military significance. In later years, he visited this and other cities that had been similarly targeted and concluded that the government's assertions of precise bombing of military targets were untrue and that large numbers of civilians had actually died.

With the support of the GI Bill, Zinn completed a doctorate in government at Columbia University and launched on an academic career. This took him, first, to Spelman College in Atlanta and then for a long tenure at Boston University. He was revered as a teacher and mentor, while he merged his university work with on-the-ground social activism and writing. He was an advisor to the Student Non-violent Coordinating Committee in its early days and took part in countless marches, protests, and demonstrations in support of the civil rights movement. He was an early and passionate opponent of the Vietnam War, seeing it as an outgrowth of colonialism that particularly affected people of color. With Daniel Berrigan, he traveled to Hanoi in 1968 to repatriate war prisoners who had been released by North Vietnam. In the years before his death,

Frederic C. Craigie, Jr., Ph.D.

Zinn similarly spoke out against the Iraq war, arguing that it violated the UN charter and caused substantial and unnecessary suffering.

Over his long career, Zinn published dozens of books and articles. He is probably best known for his 1980 *People's History of the United States*, which recounts American history from the vantage points of disenfranchised people: Native Americans, slaves, workers and early participants in union movements, women in the struggle toward suffrage, and ethnic and racial minorities. Many attempts have been made to discredit and ban the book, but it continues to sell robustly and to be widely used as a university history text.

The quotation comes from Zinn's 2006 book, *A Power Governments Cannot Suppress* (City Lights).

-50-

Hope is a state of mind, not of the world. Hope, in this deep and powerful sense, is not the same as joy that things are going well, or willingness to invest in enterprises that are obviously heading for success, but rather an ability to work for something because it is good, not because it stands a chance to succeed.

Václav Havel

For two days in the summer of 1848, 300 women and men gathered in Seneca Falls, New York for the first women's rights convention, known today as the "Seneca Falls Convention." It was organized by Elizabeth Cady Stanton and Lucretia Mott, along with Mary M'Clintock and Mott's sister, Martha Coffin Wright, all of whom had been active abolitionists and had advocated for women's rights throughout the 1840s.

The purpose of the convention was "to discuss the social, civil, and religious condition and rights of women." It apparently did indeed feature lively discussion, and it resulted in a Declaration of Rights and Sentiments, which was to be a foundational document in the history of the feminist movement in the United States. Written by Stanton and modeled on the American Declaration of Independence, it began, "We hold these truths to be self-evident; that all men *and women* are created equal; that they are endowed by their Creator with certain inalienable rights; that among these are life, liberty, and the pursuit of happiness." The first among a list of grievances was, "He [pronouns referring to men and women] has never permitted her to exercise her inalienable right to the elective franchise." The document was signed by 68 women and 32 men, including Frederick Douglass.

The Seneca Falls Convention was the first among a number of national and state women's rights conferences held in the 1850s and 1860s. These later conferences drew in additional notable women in leadership positions, including Susan B. Anthony and Lucy Stone. A state convention in Ohio in 1851 witnessed the iconic *Ain't I a Woman* speech by Sojourner Truth (who, in an intriguing sidelight of history, had been born into slavery in the north, in upstate New York and had grown up with Dutch as her first language). All of these conferences advocated for women's rights broadly—property rights, for instance—but always held a special emphasis on the long-running hope of voting rights and representation.

The public lives of all of the women who played prominent roles in the women's rights conventions were focused in the mid-to-late 19th century. Mott was the oldest among them, born in 1793. The youngest among the women I have mentioned was Susan B. Anthony, born in 1820. None of these women lived to see the ratification of the 19th Amendment, guaranteeing women the right to vote, in 1920.

Hope does not rest on the assumption or likelihood that the things that we hope *for* will come to pass. Rather, as Havel says, it is the willingness to work for something because it is good.

Nineteenth century women's rights advocates clearly were hopeful that there might someday be a world where women were treated the same as men. They were undeterred by the distance that lay between them and that horizon—and even by the fact that they would never see it themselves—and they were willing to work toward the justice of gender equality because it is good.

As is often the case, word origins are revealing. Our modern word *hope* comes most directly from the late Old English *hopa*, "confidence in the future, expectation of something desired, wishful desire." But there is also a possible etymological connection with the word *hop* (the Old English origin of which is *hoppian*, "to spring, leap; to dance") with one scholar suggesting hoping as "leaping in expectation."

To hope means to hold forth a desired outcome, to be directed and energized by a desired outcome. But is also implies… embraces… requires… action. To be hopeful means to work toward something because it matters, even in the face of uncertainty about whether it ever will come to pass.

Havel knew what he was talking about. As a dissident-turned-politician in his native Czechoslovakia, he held lifelong hopes for the dissolution of ties with Soviet communism, and for democratic, humanitarian, and environmental reforms. His path in aiming to realize these hopes was often rocky. He was frequently under surveillance by secret police, arrested multiple times, and imprisoned for as long as four years for his political activity. No doubt there were times when the horizon looked distant for him, too, but he persevered in his advocacy of progressive causes because they were good.

Frederic C. Craigie, Jr., Ph.D.

You can hold hope for whatever causes are important to you—world peace, nuclear disarmament, climate change, income inequality, health care access, civility in political discourse—or any among countless other causes, large or small. You can hold this hope and allow it to stir your soul. And you can sit with the question of what you are going to do, even without any guarantee of success or progress, because it is good.

Reflection

- What are the causes that matter to you? How distant are the horizons?

- What have you done on behalf of these causes? Particularly with causes with little visible likelihood of immanent "success," how would you put into words why it was important to you to do what you did?

- What examples occur to you—historically prominent people or people whom you have personally known—who have acted on behalf of what was important to them even as the prospects of hoped-for outcomes were small?

- During the next week, think about what you might do in the coming weeks or months in support of causes that are dear to you, building on what you have been doing, or perhaps charting some new directions.

Author

Václav Havel (1936-2011) was equal parts Czech dissident, poet and playwright, and statesman. He grew up in affluence but saw his family's fortunes fall when their property was confiscated by the communist government in 1948. He was introduced to theater when he worked as a stagehand in Prague, and he began writing his own plays in his early 20s. Havel was actively involved in the world of letters for the rest of his life, publishing over three dozen plays, collections of poetry, and works of nonfiction.

Havel was a supporter of the liberal reforms that culminated in the Prague Spring in 1968. When the Warsaw Pact countries invaded Czechoslovakia later that year to suppress the reform movement, Havel's plays (which had frequently criticized life under a totalitarian system) were banned. He was active in writing and organizing on behalf of human rights in the 1970s and 1980s, continuing his criticism of the Soviet-style communist system and of efforts in Czechoslovakia to accommodate to it. His surveillance and imprisonments took place during these years.

By the late 1980s, popular discontent with communist rule had congealed and led to massive anti-government demonstrations. Havel was the founder of the Civic Forum, bringing together dissident organizations that formed to move Czechoslovakia toward a more democratic system. When the communist party agreed to join in a coalition government with the Civic Forum in 1989, Havel was elected interim president and, subsequently, president. With the dissolution of Czechoslovakia in 1993 into the independent states of the Czech Republic and Slovakia, Havel became the first president of the Czech Republic. Havel's life after his political career saw lectureships in the United States, continued organizing and advocacy for human rights, continued writing, and widespread international recognition.

The quotation comes from Havel's 1986 book, *Disturbing the Peace*, an autobiographical reflection that grew out of conversations with Czech journalist Karel Hvizdala. It was translated and published in English in 1991 (Vintage).

Frederic C. Craigie, Jr., Ph.D.

-51-

Recent strains of activism proceed on the realization that victory is not some absolute state far away, but the achieving of it, not the moon landing but the flight... The term, "politics of prefiguration" has long been used to describe the idea that if you embody what you aspire to, you have already succeeded. That is to say, if your activism is already democratic, peaceful, creative, then in one small corner the world these things have triumphed. Activism, in this model, is not only a toolbox to change things, but a home in which to take up residence and live according to your beliefs, even if it's a temporary and local place, this paradise of participating, this vale where souls get made.

Rebecca Solnit

Building on earlier pilot programs in Canada and in his native Pittsburgh, Fred Rogers began production of his iconic *Mister Rogers' Neighborhood* for a national audience in 1968. The program continued until 2001, two years before Rogers' death.

The show helped a generation of children to feel accepted and valued and to approach the world in a spirit of wonder and compassion. Much of the conversation was about emotions, with Rogers gently and repeatedly pointing out that feelings are acceptable, and that the human challenge for children (as for the rest of us) is to learn to address feelings in positive and peaceful ways. What is mentionable, he would say, is manageable.

The show's long-running series of factory visits invited viewers' curiosity and exploration about the origins of some of the commonplace items of everyday life. How are crayons made? Graham crackers? Trumpets? Toilets? Fortune cookies? Light bulbs? Rogers would travel to local workplaces to show manufacturing processes while always featuring and highlighting the people who did the work.

Rogers was also not hesitant in addressing difficult social issues. In his characteristic gentle style, he spoke with children about topics like divorce, racial justice, mental health issues, disability rights, and war.

In 1969, against the backdrop of a series of incidents of African-American people being denied access to whites-only public swimming pools, Rogers famously invited African-American cast member François Clemmons to cool his feet next to Rogers in a small wading pool. As they shared the same towel in drying off together, Rogers commented, "Sometimes a minute like this will really make a difference." Nearly half a century later, Clemmons reflected, "I carried the hope inside of me that, one day, the world would change. And I do feel that the world still has not totally changed, but it is changing. We're getting there."

I have often thought that we in the West are obsessed with quantitative measures of success. Bigger houses are better than smaller houses. Fancier cars are better than humble ones. More members of your Twitter feed or Linkedin account are better than fewer.

Nor is the arena of caring and compassion necessarily immune from measuring success in terms of quantity. Are we not tempted to think that larger religious communities are more successful than smaller ones? That orchestrating the preservation of more acres of natural land is better than fewer? That the recipient of a multi-million-dollar research grant to study the treatment of some tropical disease is more worthy of public accolades than the person who is on the ground doing the work? That an inspirational self-help book that sells a hundred thousand copies is better than one that sells three hundred copies?

Of course, it is fine to celebrate large religious communities, the preservation of natural habitats, and advancing the science of health care. It's fine to write books that people actually read. But Solnit locates the idea of hope in a value system that disengages the linkage of success with ultimate quantifiable outcomes. If you embody what you aspire to, you have already succeeded. In one small corner of the world, the values that matter to you will have succeeded.

Fred Rogers did not broadly solve the struggle toward racial justice. But in embodying the value of treating other people with respect and dignity, he already succeeded. In touching the heart of his actor/friend, he made a difference in one small corner of the world.

Hope does not rest in broadly changing the world. If you value kindness and embody kindness, you have already succeeded. If you value economic justice and navigate your financial life in a just way, you have succeeded. If you value civil discourse, and make efforts—however halting or inelegant—to respectfully and curiously engage people who hold very different opinions, you have succeeded in your particular corner of the world.

The argument here is not an apology for a one-and-done mentality. Do explore ways to expand the influence in the world of values that are important to you. But do also recognize that small acts of goodness matter, and that the world is ultimately changed by a succession of these acts.

Reflection

- Think about the idea of "success" as embodying what you aspire to... embodying what matters to you... even without any visible outward effects. What is your reaction to this? What story from your own life experience comes to mind? Might this perspective on success cast the idea of hope in a new light?

- As we consider "visible outward effects," it is of course important to recognize that you can never fully see the results of what you do. A family doctor friend tells the story—most of us in health care have had countless experiences along these lines—of suggesting to a patient that he had serious problems with alcohol. The patient said that he felt insulted and stormed out of the room. Three years later, he came back to say how grateful he was for my friend's courage and candor and that that conversation had really marked the beginning of his road to recovery. Remember this, also, as you wonder if your efforts toward hoped-for changes make any difference.

- We can take pride and find personal satisfaction in any act that embodies what we believe. At the same time, most of us who are responsible citizens and compassionate human beings do hope to bring about some ripple effects out there of what we do. After all, it probably *is* better that Fred Rogers reached millions of children, rather than a few dozen. Can these two perspectives on hope and success—"I can find meaning in embodying what I believe" and "I can work toward change out there in the world"—coexist? Or does focusing on one of these perspectives diminish the other?

- In the week to come, notice (or create) instances of embodying what you aspire to.

Author

Rebecca Solnit (b. 1958) is an American writer and essayist. She grew up in California, pursuing an unorthodox educational track that included forgoing most of high school in favor of a GED, later finishing college and earning a master's degree in journalism.

She has produced a steady stream of books and essays since the mid-1980s, exploring a large range of topics that have tweaked her curiosity: Irish history, landscapes of the American West, Alzheimer's Disease, flora and fauna native to California, a history of walking, a cultural and historic atlas of New York City—a diverse portfolio. She published a landmark study of the reactions of communities to natural disasters, focusing particularly on the 1989 Loma Prieta earthquake and on Hurricane Katrina, in which she highlighted both the shortcomings of governmental responses and the triumph of communities working together.

Solnit became somewhat a celebrity to a younger, progressive, female readership with her 2014 *Men Explain Things to Me*, reflecting on her experiences as a woman in condescending interactions with men. Two years later, she further endeared herself to this audience. She had written

Hope in the Dark: Untold Histories, Wild Possibilities in 2004 as a reaction to what she saw as widespread demoralization about the Bush administration. Two days after the 2016 election, she posted an online invitation of a free download of the book. She had 30,000 responses in the following week. She was becoming, in the words of the *New York Times*, a "Voice of the Resistance."

The quotation appears in *Hope in the Dark* (Haymarket, 2016).

-5 2-

People say, what is the sense of our small effort? They cannot see that we must lay one brick at a time, take one step at a time. A pebble cast into a pond causes ripples that spread in all directions. Each one of our thoughts, words and deeds is like that. No one has a right to sit down and feel hopeless. There is too much work to do.

Dorothy Day

In cultivating hope, it all matters. Deeds matter. Words matter. And thoughts—the wellspring of words and deeds—matter.

It is easy to become immobilized in the face of looming challenges in the wider world and in our own lives. Most of us, I imagine, have had the experience of sitting down and feeling hopeless. The word for this is despair.

Like other packages of beliefs, behavior and emotions, that we summarily consider to be "negative"—depression, anxiety and anger are among them—despair has a dual life. On one hand, it is a painful human experience, and living in the emptiness and hollowness of despair quickly robs people of their humanity. At the same time, despair is a prompt—a loud, evolutionarily hard-wired prompt—to *do something.* It is painful, and it is useful because it can stir us toward meaningful action.

Lingering in despair, being captured by despair, serves no one. Being able to look beyond the suffering of despair to see the message that it brings prompts soul-enlivening action. The cure for despair, organizational consultant Margaret Wheatley says, "is discovering what we want to do about something we care about."

Dorothy Day certainly knew this well. Her entire adult life was devoted to causes that were, shall we say, outside of the mainstream of popular opinion. In her late teens, she was jailed for demonstrating on behalf of women's suffrage. As a young adult, Day read Tolstoy and Upton Sinclair and was closely involved with people who were active in anarchist and communist movements and with the International Workers of the World—the I.W.W, the Wobblies. After her conversion to Catholicism in the late 1920s, Day was always a faithful member of the larger Church, while being unafraid to advocate for positions that put her at odds with Church leadership. She opposed nationalist general Francisco Franco during the Spanish Civil War. She supported child labor laws and worker strikes that the Catholic hierarchy opposed. She was an ardent pacifist and rejected the just-war position of the American church and almost exclusively of the American public.

Rather than lingering in despair about the tenuous prospects of unpopular causes, Day set to work. She cofounded the *Catholic Worker,* commenting on the life of the Church and social justice, and served as its editor for 47 years until her death in 1980. She founded several dozen settlement houses and Catholic Worker communities in the United States, Canada, and the United Kingdom. She wrote celebrated books of autobiography. She engaged acts of civil disobedience and traveled internationally into her 70s.

Day's experience, at least that which I'm describing here, concerns her advocacy for large societal issues. But the relationship of despair and hope plays out with individuals, as well. I have lost count of the number of people who have commented along the lines of a man with late-stage colon cancer; "My illness, all of the sadness of my illness, has been the worst experience of my life. But you know, it's also been the best experience of my life; it's made me look at how I was living and helped me to see more clearly than ever what's important and what's not, and I've been devoting whatever time I may have to loving the people around me and loving myself. I guess it's made me a real person."

Or in my seasonal home in Tucson. In the wake of the tragic sudden death of their 3-year-old son Ben, his mother Jeannette Maré, and her husband were both devastated and also touched by the support and kindness of people around them. With friends, they began crafting ceramic bells symbolizing kindness, hanging them around their home and distributing them in the community. Kindness, they decided, was at the heart of their healing journey, and this has evolved as the focal point of *Ben's Bells*, a major initiative in encouraging and gathering stories of kindness that has now engaged over 25,000 people. Out of the despair and unspeakable pain of their loss has come a project that, as Jeannette describes it, "will touch others' lives and help to make our community a gentler place to live."

In the setting of suffering, in the setting of loss, in the setting of injustice, the human experience of despair asks the question, "How, now, are you going to live your life?" The answer, whether or not the world or the circumstances are visibly changed, lights the pathway toward hope.

Frederic C. Craigie, Jr., Ph.D.

Reflection

- When have you experienced despair? How have you reacted to despair—in deeds, words and thoughts—that has stirred your soul in some way?

- In what ways, now, do you feel despair? When you think about whatever circumstances you're facing; what does Day's idea of "work to do" mean to you?

- Even in the absence of life-compromising illness or tragic losses, have you had some experience where something was painful and also helped you to chart more enlivening and meaningful directions?

- In the coming week, notice times when you begin to feel an absence of hope or a sense of despair. Consider that feeling as a prompt toward meaningful action. What form will "work to do" take?

Author

Dorothy Day (1897-1980) was a writer, activist, and social reformer. She was born in New York and moved with her family to Oakland, California in 1904. Her father worked for a newspaper whose offices were destroyed in the 1906 earthquake, and Day's observations of people helping one another in the wake of the devastation helped to form her understanding of the healing effects of community. She moved back to New York in her late teens, living in Greenwich Village, working as a journalist, and finding a home in a counter-cultural literary and political scene. Day joined the Catholic church in 1927 and for the rest of her life, remained grounded in Catholic faith and practice while urging the church in progressive directions. In addition to her regular writing for the *Catholic Worker*, Day published seven books, the most widely circulated being the autobiographical *The Long Loneliness* (Harper and Brothers, 1952). As late as her mid-seventies, Day traveled around the United States and internationally, meeting fellow reformers and activists, including Mother Teresa and Cesar Chavez.

In 2015, Pope Francis addressed a joint session of Congress and cited Day as one of four exemplary people who had made a profound impact on the spiritual and social history of America. The others were Abraham Lincoln, Martin Luther King Jr., and Thomas Merton.

The quotation comes from *Singing the Living Tradition* (Unitarian Universalist Association, 1993).

The quotation from Meg Wheatley comes from her lovely short book, *Turning to One Another: Simple Conversations to Restore Hope to the Future* (Berrett-Koehler, 2009). The quotation from Jeannette Maré, comes from the Ben's Bells website, https://bensbells.org/, which has information about Ben, the history of the project, reflections on kindness as an intentional practice, and personal stories of the bells as prompts for kindness from around the world.

Frederic C. Craigie, Jr., Ph.D.

Afterword

Dear Reader:

Thanks for coming along on the journey. I hope it has been as meaningful for you reading the book as it certainly has been for me getting the book together.

When I read or peruse books, I try to identify one or two key ideas that I want to hold onto and carry forward. As you think about your exploration of these meditations and themes, what might be key ideas for you? What has been affirmed for you, or what has been new? In what ways might your understanding of yourself and the world be a little wider than it was before? Which chapters particularly resonated with you? What qualities and values about living your life have you always held that you may hope to embody even more fully on the road ahead?

Let me invite you to sit with these questions. As you do, remember that it is your wisdom, more than mine, and the truth that you hold in your own heart that ultimately makes for "meaningful, peaceful and joyful living."

Let me also invite you to visit my website, www.goodnessofheart.com. In addition to lovely Maine images, you'll find a posting of my weekly reflections, a periodic blog, lots of print and web-based resources, and information and excerpts from my earlier book, *Positive Spirituality in Health*

Frederic C. Craigie, Jr., Ph.D.

Care: Nine Practical Approaches to Pursuing Wholeness for Clinicians, Patients, and Health Care Organizations (Mill City Press, 2010).

You'll also find my current email contact information. I'm always happy to hear from readers and delighted to continue the conversation about these sacred human qualities that we've explored together. Feel welcome and encouraged to write. Oh, and I'll be more likely to pick up your email amid all the others that come in every day if you write "Weekly Soul" in the subject line.

And now, as we close, let me leave you with the blessing that I have shared with many groups in addresses and ceremonies:

- May you go forth affirmed, and challenged, and renewed.

- May you remember who you are and who you are called to be.

- May you always find beauty and wonder in the sacred space around you.

- May you care for and love yourself as you care for and love other people on the journey of healing and aliveness and fullness of life.

Sources

Miracles

1. As I indicate in the text, the provenance of this familiar quotation from Albert Einstein is not completely clear. The most direct pathway is that it is cited in Hinshaw, RE (2006), *Living with Nature's Extremes: The Life of Gilbert Fowler White*. Boulder, CO: Johnson Books, quoting White in his book, now long out of print, *Journal of France and Germany (1942-1944)*.

2. Cather, W. (1927). *Death Comes to the Archbishop*. New York: Alfred A. Knopf. This is the original publication; Cather's book has been re-published numerous times over the years.

3. Nepo, M. (2011). *The Book of Awakening*. San Francisco: Conari Press.

4. Keller, H. (1903). *Optimism*. New York: T. Y. Crowell and Company. Like Cather's book, Keller's essay has been re-printed many times in various venues. Edith Pagelson's story, written in collaboration with my colleague and friend Ronnie Weston, is available in

Frederic C. Craigie, Jr., Ph.D.

Against All Odds: A Miracle of Holocaust Survival (Rockland, Maine: Maine Authors Publishing, 2012).

Aliveness

5. Like Einstein's quotation, the quotation from Howard Thurman is often-cited but lacks a single, specific source. The Howard Thurman Center for Common Ground at Boston University attests to the provenance of this quotation with Thurman, saying that he was a sought-after speaker and undoubtedly spoke these words on multiple occasions. One confirmed source is "The Sound of the Genuine," a baccalaureate address that Thurman presented at Spelman College in 1980. You can see excerpts presented by *DailyGood* at http://www.dailygood. org/story/1846/the-sound-of-the-genuine-howard-thurman/.

6. Shea, J. (2000). *Spirituality and Health Care: Reaching Toward a Holistic Future.* Chicago: The Park Ridge Center for the Study of Health, Faith and Ethics.

7. Campbell, J, with Moyers, B. (1991). *The Power of Myth.* New York: Anchor Books.

8. The William Sloane Coffin quotation comes from an interview, two years before his death, with journalist Bob Abernethy on the PBS program, *Religion and Ethics Newsweekly.* See https://www.pbs.org/wnet/religionandethics/2004/08/27/august-27-2004-william-sloane-coffin-extended-interview/2945/.

9. Rubin, BM. (1998). *Fifty on Fifty: Wisdom, Inspiration, and Reflections on Women's Lives Well Lived.* New York: Warner Books.

Purpose

10. Muller, W. (1996). *How, Then, Shall We Live? Four Simple Questions the Reveal the Beauty and Meaning of Our Lives.* New York: Bantam.

11. The David Whyte quotation comes from an interview, titled "Making Work Meaningful: Towards a Soul-based Workplace," aired on the PBS program, *Body & Soul with Gail Harris.* See https://www.pbs.org/bodyandsoul/216/whyte.htm.

12. Brooks, D. (2015). *The Road to Character.* New York: Random House.

13. The often-cited comment from Miles Davis is variously quoted both as "play like yourself" and "sound like yourself." I suspect that Davis phrased the idea both ways multiple times. The "sound like yourself" version appears in a book of essays from Pulitzer-prize-winning poet W. D. Snodgrass, titled (appropriately) *To Sound Like Yourself* (BOA Editions Ltd., 2002).

14. McKay, M, Forsyth, J, and Eifert, G. (2010). *Your Life on Purpose: How to Find What Matters and Create the Life You Want.* Oakland, CA: New Harbinger.

Laughter and Joy

15. The quotation from Frederic and Mary Ann Brussat is posted in their review of Mark Nepo's 2005 book, *The Exquisite Risk.* See https://www.spiritualityandpractice.com/book-reviews/view/9562/the-exquisite-risk.

16. Dossey, L. (2001). *Healing Beyond the Body: Medicine and the Infinite Reach of the Mind.* Boston: Shambhala.

17. Pierce, LB. (2003). *Simplicity Lessons: A 12-Step Guide to Living Simply.* Carmel, CA: Gallagher Press.

18. Peterson, C. (2006). *A Primer in Positive Psychology.* New York: Oxford University Press.

Presence

19. Kornfield, J. (1993). *A Path with Heart: A Guide Through the Perils and Promises of Spiritual Life.* New York: Bantam.

20. Chopra, D. (1993). *Ageless Body, Timeless Mind: The Quantum Alternative to Growing Old.* New York: Harmony Books.

21. Merton, T. (1968). *Conjectures of a Guilty Bystander.* Garden City, NY: Image Books.

22. Beattie, M. (1996). *Journey to the Heart: Daily Meditations on the Path to Freeing Your Soul.* San Francisco: HarperSanFrancisco.

23. Norris, G. (1992). *Sharing Silence: Meditation Practice and Mindful Living.* New York: Bell Tower.

Activism

24. The Terkel quotation comes from the December 19, 2003 broadcast of the PBS program, *Religion & Ethics Newsweekly.* See https://www.pbs.org/wnet/religionandethics/2003/12/19/december-19-2003-interview-studs-terkel/11022/.

25. Palmer, P. (2000). *Let Your Life Speak: Listening for the Voice of Vocation.* San Francisco: Jossey-Bass.

26. Schlitz, MM, Vieten, C, and Amorok, T. (2007). *Living Deeply: The Art & Science of Transformation in Everyday Life.* Oakland, CA: New Harbinger.

27. Tippett, K. (2016). *Becoming Wise: An Inquiry into the Mystery and Art of Living.* New York: Penguin.

Acceptance

28. Sanderson C, and Linehan, MM, (1999). Acceptance and Forgiveness. In WR Miller (Ed.), *Integrating Spirituality into Treatment: Resources for Practitioners.* Washington, DC: American Psychological Association.

29. Hayes, SC, with Smith, S. (2005). *Get out of Your Mind and into Your Life: The New Acceptance and Commitment Therapy.* Oakland, CA: New Harbinger.

30. Frankl, VE. (2006). *Man's Search for Meaning.* Boston: Beacon Press.

31. Berry, W. (1983). *Standing by Words.* Berkeley, CA: Counterpoint.

32. Roosevelt, E. (1960). *You Learn by Living: Eleven Keys to a More Fulfilling Life.* New York: Harper & Row.

Gratitude

33. Steindl-Rast, D. (1984). *Gratefulness, the Heart of Prayer.* Ramsey, NJ: Paulist Press.

34. Kushner, H. (1995). God's Fingerprints on the Soul. In R Carlson and B Shield (Eds.), *Handbook for the Soul.* Boston: Little, Brown and Company.

35. Schweitzer, A. (1975). *Thoughts for our Times.* White Plains, NY: Peter Pauper Press.

36. The Emmons quotation comes from his 2013 essay, "How Gratitude Can Help You Through Hard Times," posted in *DailyGood.* See http://www.dailygood.org/

story/532/how-gratitude-can-help-you-through-hard-times-robert-emmons/.

Forgiveness

37. Walsch, ND. (1999). Foreword. In J. Jampolsky, *Forgiveness: The Greatest Healer of All.* Hillsboro, OR: Beyond Words Publishing.

38. Nerburn, K. (1999). *Make Me an Instrument of Your Peace: Living in the Spirit of the Prayer of St. Francis.* New York: HarperOne.

39. Germer, C. (2009). *The Mindful Path to Self-Compassion: Freeing Yourself from Destructive Thoughts and Emotions.* New York: Guilford Press.

40. Tutu, DM. and Tutu, MA. (2014). *The Book of Forgiving: The Fourfold Path for Healing Ourselves and Our World.* New York: HarperCollins.

Creativity

41. Korn, P. (2013). *Why We Make Things and Why it Matters: The Education of a Craftsman.* Jaffrey, NH: David R. Godine.

42. Wakefield, W. (2001). *Releasing the Creative Spirit.* Woodstock, VT: SkyLight Paths.

43. The quotation from Ms. Fitzgerald is undated and appears on the website of the Ella Fitzgerald Charitable Foundation. See http://www.ellafitzgerald.com/about/quotes.

44. The quotation from Charlie Parker is cited in Reisner, R. (1977). *Bird: The Legend of Charlie Parker.* Boston: Da Capo Press.

Civility

45. The quotation from Dr. King comes from his sermon, *Loving your Enemies,* delivered on November 17, 1957, at the Dexter Avenue Baptist Church, in Montgomery, Alabama. It is presented in full text as part of a collection of eleven of Dr. King's speeches at a website maintained by a public library in Illinois. See http://www.richtonparklibrary.org/images/ stories/pdfs/2013/MLK-2014/MLK-Speeches-Eleven-65pp.pdf. The text of the sermon itself, minus some introductory words that are included in the Richton Park version, is available in print form: Carson, C. and Holloran, P. (Eds.). (1998). *A Knock at Midnight: Inspiration from the Great Sermons of Reverend Martin Luther King, Jr.* New York: Warner Books.

46. Hanh, TN. (2005). *Being Peace.* Berkeley, CA: Parallax Press.

47. Rosen, M. (1998). *Thank You for Being Such a Pain: Spiritual Guidance for Dealing with Difficult People.* New York: Three Rivers Press.

48. Williamson, M. (2004). *The Gift of Change: Spiritual Guidance for a Radically New Life.* New York: HarperCollins.

Hope

49. Zinn, H. (2006). *A Power Governments Cannot Suppress.* San Francisco: City Lights.

50. The quotation comes from Havel's 1986 book, *Disturbing the Peace,* an autobiographical reflection that grew out of conversations with Czech journalist

Karel Hvizdala. It was translated and published in English in 1991 (New York: Vintage Books).

51. Solnit, R. (2016). *Hope in the Dark*. Chicago: Haymarket Books.

52. The quotation from Dorothy Day appears as Reading #560 in *Singing the Living Tradition* (Boston: Unitarian Universalist Association, 1993).

About the Author

Frederic Craigie Ph.D. is a clinical psychologist, consultant, educator, speaker, and writer. His passions and areas of expertise include spirituality in health and health care, healing relationships, clinician well-being, and resiliency and positive mental health.

Fred attended Dartmouth College during the tumultuous Vietnam War era and completed his doctorate at the University of Utah. He served internships in the VA system in clinical psychology and in substance abuse rehabilitation. Following his training, he began what was to become a 37-year full-time faculty role at the Maine -Dartmouth Family Medicine Residency in Augusta, Maine, where he coordinated behavioral health teaching for residents and students and provided behavioral health care to a largely underserved primary care population.

He serves as Visiting Associate Professor at the Andrew Weil Center for Integrative Medicine (AWCIM) at the University of Arizona College of Medicine, and held an appointment as Associate Professor of Community and Family Medicine at the Geisel School of Medicine at Dartmouth until his "semi-retirement" in 2015.

Since the mid-eighties, Fred has written and presented extensively about the healing and life-giving roles of spirituality in health and patient care, in the experience of health care providers, and in the life and culture of healthcare organizations. He received a John Templeton Spirituality and Medicine Award for Primary Care Residency Training Programs (in conjunction with George Washington University Medical Center, Institute for Spirituality and Health) in 2002. He takes particular joy in having founded the *Tom Nevola, M.D. Symposium on Spirituality and Health*, the oldest academic symposium on spiritual-

Frederic C. Craigie, Jr., Ph.D.

ity and health in the United States. He is also the founder of a spiritual care program at the Residency's affiliated hospital and served for many years as associate editor of a professional journal devoted to Christian faith and mental health.

With AWCIM, Fred has developed curricula and taught about spirituality, healing relationships, leadership, and clinician wellness and self-care in the Center's programs for fellows, allied health professionals, students, and for the general public.

He is the author of *Positive Spirituality in Health Care: Nine Practical Approaches to Pursuing Wholeness for Clinicians, Patients, and Health Care Organizations*, (Mill City Press, 2010).

Fred also serves on the Board of Directors of Community Health Options in Lewiston, Maine. CHO is a nonprofit, member-directed, co-op health insurance company that was formed with the inception of the ACA and continues to provide health care access to a substantial population of largely underserved and self-employed Mainers.

His website, offering a variety of resources, a periodic blog, and weekly reflections on spirituality and health, is www.goodnessofheart.com.

In his personal life, Fred cherishes his relationships with his wife, grown children and grandchildren, extended family, and friends. His own approach to "meaningful, joyful and peaceful living" also includes regular spiritual reflection and practice, along with playing fiddle and mandolin, running up and down the court playing basketball, doing carpentry and home projects, being sure to laugh regularly, and resolutely following the subtleties and wonders of major league baseball. He has called Maine "home" since the mid-seventies and now lives seasonally in Tucson.

Select MSI Books

Inspirational, Philosophical, and Spiritual Books

A Believer-in-Waiting's First Encounters with God (Mahlou)

A Guide to Bliss (Tubali)

Blest Atheist (Mahlou)

Christmas at the Mission (Sula)

Dia de Muertos (Sula)

Easter at the Mission (Sula)

El Poder de lo Transpersonal (Ustman)

Everybody's Little Book of Everyday Prayers (MacGregor)

God Speaks into Darkness (Easterling)

How My Cat Made Me a Better Man (Feig)

How to Argue with an Atheist (Brink)

Introductory Lectures on Religious Philosophy (Sabzevary)

Jesus Is Still Passing By (Easterling)

Joshuanism (Tosto)

Living in Blue Sky Mind (Diedrichs)

Of God, Rattlesnakes, and Okra (Easterling)

One Family: Indivisible (Greenebaum)

One Simple Text... (Shaw & Brown)

Overcoming the Odds (C. Leaver)

Passing On (Romer)

Puertas a la Eternidad (Ustman)

Rainstorm of Tomorrow (Dong)

Road Map to Power (A. Husain & D. Husain)

Saints I Know (Sula)

Surviving Cancer, Healing People: One Cat's Story (Sula)

The Seven Wisdoms of Life (Tubali)

SELF-HELP BOOKS

100 Tips and Tools for Managing Chronic Illness (Charnas)

A Woman's Guide to Self-Nurturing (Romer)

Creative Aging (Vassiliadis & Romer)

Divorced! (Romer)

Harnessing the Power of Grief (Potter)

Healing from Incest (Henderson & Emerton)

Helping the Disabled Veteran (Romer)

He's a Porn Addict...Now What? (Overbay & Shea)

How to Get Happy and Stay That Way (Romer)

How to Live from Your Heart (Hucknall)

Life after Losing a Child (Young & Romer)

Living Well with Chronic Illness (Charnas)

Sula and the Franciscan Sisters (Sula)

Survival of the Caregiver (Snyder)

Tale of a Mission Cat (Sula)

The Rise and Fall of Muslim Civil Society (O. Imady)

The Rose and the Sword (Bach & Hucknall)

When You're Shoved from the Right, Look to Your Left (O. Imady)

OUR PANDEMIC SERIES BOOKS
BY EXPERTS TO MANAGE THE PANDEMIC

10 Quick Homework Tips (Alder & Trombly)

Awesome Couple Communication (Pickett)

Choice and Structure for Children with Autism (McNeil)

Diary of an RVer during Quarantine (MacDonald)

Exercising in a Pandemic (Young)

God Speaks into Darkness (Easterling)

How to Stay Calm in Chaos (Gentile)

Old and On Hold (Cooper)

Parenting in a Pandemic (Bayarddelle)

Porn and the Pandemic (Shea)

Seeking Balance in an Unbalanced Time (Greenebaum)

Staying Safe While Sheltering in Place (Schnuelle, Adams, & Henderson)

The Marriage Whisperer (Pickett)

The Optimistic Food Addict (Fisanick)

The Pandemic and Hope (Ortman)

Tips, Tools, and Anecdotes to Help during a Pandemic (Charnas)

Women, We're Only Old Once (Cooper)

CPSIA information can be obtained
at www.ICGtesting.com
Printed in the USA
BVHW030741020921
615647BV00006B/21